A Quilter's Ark

More than 50 Designs for Foundation Piecing

Margaret Rolfe

ACKNOWLEDGMENTS

I have many people to thank for helping me with this book. Ann-Maree Jacobs really made it all happen, with her insistence that my designs should be put into foundation piecing. She has been wonderfully helpful and enthusiastic from beginning to end. I am grateful to all the Canberra Quilters who tried out designs for me, and I especially appreciate those who contributed their finished blocks to the book. I must thank Becky Peters, whose thoughtful criticism gave me important insights into foundation piecing. My friends helped by being understanding when I needed time and space to single-mindedly work.

My family rallied around to help, and my son Phil again contributed a beautiful animal drawing for the title page. Melinda, my daughter, was invaluable in many ways—sewing, drawing, criticizing, and advising, not to mention cooking dinners and feeding the pets! Finally, none of this would be possible without the enthusiastic support and encouragement of my husband, Barry, whose motto is "Never, ever give up!"

Library of Congress Cataloging-in-Publication Data

Rolfe, Margaret
    A quilter's ark : more than 50 designs for foundation piecing / Margaret Rolfe.
       p. cm.
      ISBN 1-56477-197-0
      1. Patchwork—Patterns. 2. Appliqué—Patterns.
3. Patchwork quilts. 4. Animals in art.
    TT835.R65 1997
      746.46'041—dc21   97-23693
                                CIP

CREDITS

Editor-in-Chief . . . . Kerry I. Smith
Technical Editor . . . . Melissa A. Lowe
Managing Editor . . . . Judy Petry
Copy Editor . . . . Tina Cook
Proofreader . . . . Leslie Phillips
Design Director . . . . Cheryl Stevenson
Text Designer . . . . Kay Green
Cover Designer . . . . Magrit Baurecht
Production Assistant . . . . Marijane E. Figg
Illustrators . . . . Laurel Strand, Robin Strobel
Photographer . . . . Brent Kane

A Quilter's Ark:
More Than 50 Designs for Foundation Piecing
©1997 by Margaret Rolfe

That Patchwork Place, Inc., PO Box 118
Bothell, WA 98041-0118 USA

Printed in Hong Kong
02 01 00 99 98 97   6 5 4 3 2 1

> MISSION STATEMENT
>
> *We are dedicated to providing quality*
> *products and service by working together*
> *to inspire creativity and to enrich*
> *the lives we touch.*

CONTENTS

INTRODUCTION 4
HOW TO USE THIS BOOK 4
MATERIALS AND EQUIPMENT 4
    Fabric 4
    Interfacing 4
    Fusible Web 5
    Embroidery Floss 5
    Batting 5
    Pencil, Ruler, and Paper Clips 5
    Basic Sewing Supplies 5
    Miscellaneous Supplies 5
CHOOSING FABRICS 5
FOUNDATION PIECING 6
CONSTRUCTING THE BLOCKS 7
ADDING BACKGROUND STRIPS AND BORDERS 10
ADDING DETAILS 11
    Using Fusible Web for Appliqué 11
    Making Tails 11
    Embroidery 12
TURNING YOUR BLOCKS INTO QUILTS 14
    Assembling the Quilt Top 14
    Adding Borders 15
    Quilting 16
    Binding 16
GALLERY 17
BLOCKS
    Bald Eagle 49
    Beaver 50
    Black Bear 51
    Blue Jay 52
    Buffalo (Bison) 53
    Butterfly 54
    Camel 55
    Canada Goose 56
    Cardinal 57
    Cat 58
    Chick 59
    Cow 60
    Dog 61
    Dolphin 62
    Donkey 63
    Duck 64
    Duckling 65
    Elephant 66
    Emu 67
    Flamingo 68
    Giraffe 69

    Goat 70
    Hen 71
    Hippopotamus 72
    Horned Owl 73
    Hummingbird 74
    Kangaroo 75
    Koala 76
    Kookaburra 77
    Leopard 78
    Lion 79
    Loon 80
    Monkey 81
    Panda 82
    Parrot (Crimson Rosella) 83
    Peacock 84
    Pelican 85
    Penguin 86
    Pig 87
    Platypus 88
    Polar Bear 89
    Puffin 90
    Rabbit 91
    Rhinoceros 92
    Rooster 93
    Scotty Dog 94
    Sheep 95
    Tiger 96
    Tortoise 97
    Toucan 98
    Turkey 99
    Wombat 100
    Zebra 101
QUILTS
    Ark Quilt 102
    Farm Quilt 106
    North American Animals Quilt 107
    Australian Animals Quilt 108
DESIGNING QUILTS WITH ANIMAL BLOCKS 109
    Using Single Blocks 109
    Using Repetition 110
    Combining Blocks with
       Other Patchwork 110
    Combining Different
       Animal Blocks 110
METRIC CONVERSION 111
MEET THE AUTHOR 112

INTRODUCTION

*"It is our task in our time and in our
generation to hand down undiminished to
those who come after us, as was handed
down to us by those who went before, the
natural wealth and beauty which is ours."*
John Fitzgerald Kennedy (1917–1963)

I love to design pieced bird and animal blocks and
have been doing so for more than a decade. It was a
logical step to extend my designs to foundation piecing, the potential for which other people saw long
before I did. Thanks to their encouragement, I adapted
my block designs into a small size for foundation
piecing.

The blocks in this book finish to 4" x 4" or smaller,
so the foundation method is ideal (though I still prefer
to use my straight-line piecing methods for larger
blocks). One of the advantages of foundation piecing
is that you can sew small pieces easily and accurately.
I try to eliminate tiny pieces if I can, so if they remain
in a design, they are essential to making it work.

Another advantage is speed. You really can "sew and
go" with these blocks—trace the design onto the foundation, then away to the sewing machine to stitch it
up. In a very short time, you have a block you can
finish into a little quilt.

This book contains more than fifty animal designs,
so it is no accident that it is called "A Quilter's Ark."
With all these animals and birds, it is indeed an ark!
Stories can tell great truths, and the story of Noah and
his ark may be relevant to our own time. We, like Noah
and his family, hold the fate of all the animals and birds
in our hands. We need to ask ourselves, What will I do
with that responsibility? Will the tiger, snow leopard,
African elephant, and giant panda—to name only a few
endangered species—be just stories for our great-great-
grandchildren?

HOW TO USE THIS BOOK

The main feature of this book is the foundation-
piecing patterns: fifty-three animal blocks. You can use
these quick and easy blocks in many different ways.
Stitch groups of blocks together to make small theme
quilts like the Farm Quilt on page 106 or the Zoo Quilt
shown on page 48 (these make wonderful quilts for
babies and children). Try making little quilts from single
blocks—these have lots of possibilities. Make a special
gift for someone with a favorite animal, as in Miaow
Cats on page 19; celebrate holidays with an appropri-
ate animal, such as the Turkey quilt on page 34 for
Thanksgiving; or make a statement about things you
care about, as in Share the Earth on page 24. The blocks
are ideal for incorporating into clothing. Most of all,
have fun. You may want to try using blocks humorously,
as I did in I Never Saw a Purple Cow on page 22, a
poem I enjoyed as a child.

I have included patterns for four quilts on pages
102–8, or look at "Designing Quilts with Animal Blocks"
on pages 109–10 for ideas. If you would like more information on designing quilts with animal blocks, look
for my previous books, *Go Wild with Quilts* and *Go Wild
with Quilts—Again*, also from That Patchwork Place.

MATERIALS AND EQUIPMENT

Fabric

Generally, you need only small pieces of fabric for
these blocks and small quilts. I now keep all kinds of
scraps that I used to throw away. If possible, choose
all-cotton fabrics that are not too heavy in weight. For
more information on choosing colors and fabric, see
page 5.

Interfacing

The key to making these blocks is the foundation
material. Use lightweight, nonwoven, nonfusible interfacing. Interfacing is ideal because it is both sheer and
strong. You can trace your design directly onto it, then
sew and press. The interfacing will keep its shape
through sewing and pressing. Also, you do NOT need

to remove it after sewing, as you would with a paper foundation. I do not enjoy the fiddly and time-consuming job of getting out all those tiny bits of paper!

You can purchase interfacing at fabric stores that sell dressmaking supplies. Make sure that it is lightweight and nonfusible.

Fusible Web

You need small scraps of fusible web for adding appliqué details to some of the designs, such as the combs and wattles on the Rooster and Hen blocks.

Embroidery Floss

For the animals and birds shown in this book, I used embroidery floss to add details like facial features and tails.

Batting

Use very thin batting or a layer of flannel as the middle layer of your quilt. Thinner battings work better for machine quilting, which I recommend for these blocks.

Pencil, Ruler, and Paper Clips

For tracing, you need a soft (number 2 or softer) pencil, a ruler, and paper clips. Keep the pencil sharp, so that lines are crisp and dark. Use several paper clips to attach the foundation interfacing on top of the design while you trace.

Basic Sewing Supplies

You need a sewing machine (though blocks may be sewn by hand), pins, needles, scissors (a medium-size pair of scissors is ideal), seam ripper (we all make mistakes), rotary cutter and mat, quilting rulers (small rulers are especially useful), and an iron.

You also need crewel needles, which have a larger eye than regular needles, for embroidery.

Miscellaneous Supplies

You may want a spray bottle of water (to help press the seams nice and flat) and a little gadget called a "loop turner," which is useful for turning thin tubes of fabric right side out when making tails.

CHOOSING FABRICS

Working with small blocks and foundation piecing is a little different from making full-size quilts with regular methods. Following are some considerations to take into account when choosing fabrics. I do not want to be categorical about any of this. Rather, I want to warn you of some factors I have found important. In the end, trust your eye. If you think it works, then it works.

Print scale. Because the blocks are small, each print has less area in which to "establish" itself, and therefore large-scale prints must be used with care. Small-scale prints and tone-on-tone prints are especially useful in these small blocks. (I particularly enjoy using the reproduction fabrics that are now available.) However, this does not mean that large-scale prints cannot be used; they often add vibrancy to a design. For example, look at the background of Robyn Oats's Elephant block on page 42 and the border of the Toucan block on page 23.

Directional prints. Directional prints include stripes, checks, and any design with an obvious one-way pattern. Generally, directional prints are best avoided. With the flip-and-sew technique that is fundamental to foundation piecing, it can be surprisingly difficult to predict (and therefore to control) where a directional print will go after you sew it in place.

However, do use directional fabrics when you want a particular effect. Stripes are essential for tigers and zebras! Where a directional fabric is required, the block tracing diagram has a striped fill or is marked with arrows to help you position your fabric.

Value. *Value* means how light or dark a fabric is, and it is an important aspect of fabric choice. Value is relative; the same fabric may be a light value in one situation but a dark value in another, depending on the value of neighboring fabrics. With these animal designs, it is usually best to have a clear difference in value between the animal and the background. Otherwise, the animal, or part of the animal, may disappear into the background.

Color. The main thing to consider is not how a color looks on its own, but how it will interact with those around it. Also keep in mind the effect of using small pieces. A color that looks strong or bright in a larger piece can look dull in a small piece. Often, a really bright fabric is necessary to show the color you want in a small piece.

FOUNDATION PIECING

Welcome to the back-to-front world of foundation piecing! So what is foundation piecing? It is a style of pieced patchwork in which the patches, the pieces of fabric, are sewn onto a base or foundation. And why is foundation piecing a back-to-front world? There are two reasons. First, the patchwork is sewn on one side of the foundation material, but the block develops on the other. Second, the finished block design will face opposite the traced design. For instance, you would trace the elephant so that he faces to the right, but in the finished block, he would face left.

You construct the animal blocks by foundation-piecing sections of the design, then joining the sections. Before you begin, note these general points:

Remember that the finished block will be a mirror image of the traced pattern. The illustration of the finished block shows the direction of your finished block (facing left or right). If you want to change the direction, reverse the tracing as described in step 1 on page 7.

Transfer all letters, numbers, and details such as eyes and ears when tracing the pattern. You will be glad you marked the details when you want to embroider the block. Each piece is numbered according to the piecing order. Sections are labeled by letters: A, B, C, and so on. The dashed lines indicate the ¼"-wide seam allowance around each section.

Follow the numbers when adding pieces. The pieces in the tracing diagrams are numbered to indicate piecing order. Begin at number one, then follow the numbers through the block.

Work with chunks of fabric. It can be hard to cut the fabric pieces because it is difficult to predict exactly how much you need for sewing and flipping. It is much easier to cut the fabric into big chunks about 6" x 9". Place the chunk of fabric on the foundation, then sew, flip, press, and trim the excess. Use the remaining chunk for all pieces requiring that particular fabric; it will get progressively smaller. I find I waste a lot less time and fabric by working this way, rather than by trying to prejudge the size of a lot of individual patches. Save large scraps and use them for little pieces in the design.

Forget fabric grain. One of the advantages of foundation piecing is that you do not have to worry about fabric grain. It is difficult to match up the fabric grain using this technique, and since the foundation prevents stretching and ensures accuracy, why bother?

Sew on the traced side of the foundation. The patchwork will grow on the other side. For clarity, I refer to the "traced" side and the "patchwork" side throughout the book.

Sew with the machine needle in the center position. The center position gives the best visibility for following the traced line. Use a slightly smaller than usual stitch length—between 2 and 2½—but not so small that you cannot pick the stitches out if necessary.

After stitching, trim seam allowances to ⅛". Trim immediately after sewing, being careful to trim only the seam allowances and not the foundation.

Leave generous seam allowances around *unsewn* edges. After a patch has been sewn, flipped, and pressed, leave a generous ½" around the unsewn edges. You will be grateful to have the extra when you trim the seam allowances around the block.

Follow the piecing order when joining the finished sections. The animal blocks are made in sections, then joined. In the directions, a plus sign indicates a seam. When the directions say A + B, sew section A to section B. Once joined, the sections become a unit referred to as "(A-B)." The order for sewing the sections is given as a series of steps that looks like this:

1. A + B
2. (A-B) + C
3. (A-C) + D

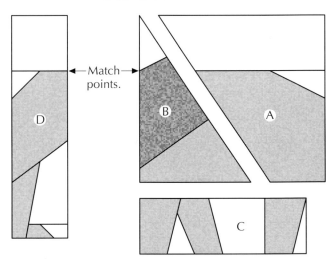

Before sewing, trim the seam allowances of sections that will be joined to ¼". It is important to trim the seam allowances *just before you join the pieced sections.*

Align sections with "match points." Some tracing diagrams have match points as shown above. You must accurately match sections at these points, or the animal design will not be properly formed. To line up sections at a match point, push a pin through both sections and align the cut edges before sewing.

Press open seams that join sections. This keeps the block nice and flat; otherwise, the bulk of the fabric-plus-interfacing makes lumps.

Some inaccuracy seems to be inevitable due to the thickness of the fabrics and the small block size. Blocks may be up to about ⅛" smaller on one or two sides when finished. This should not create a problem; just trim the block to the required size, *adjusting so you do not trim the animal design* or add a little extra to any strips or the block border (see page 10).

CONSTRUCTING THE BLOCKS

1. Cut a 7" x 7" square of interfacing. You may want to use paper clips to attach the interfacing to the page. With a ruler and a pencil, trace the animal design. Remember to trace the details.

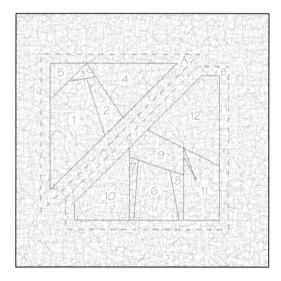

To make a *reverse block* (with the animal or bird facing the opposite direction), trace the design onto interfacing, but do not copy the numbers. Turn the interfacing over, retrace the lines if necessary (to make them clear), then copy the numbers. To remind myself that the block is reversed, I mark an *R* on the edge of each section.

2. Cut the interfacing into sections, cutting outside the dashed lines as shown.

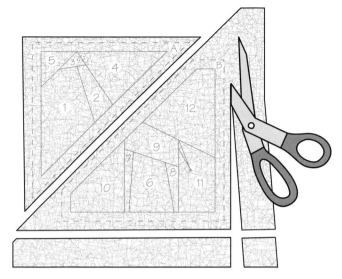

3. Cut a piece of fabric to cover piece 1, including a generous ½" for seam allowances. Place the fabric, right side up, on what will become the patchwork side of the interfacing. Piece 1 is like the center of a Log Cabin block; it is the only piece you put right side up. *Note:* For clarity, the illustrations show the block from the traced side of the foundation.

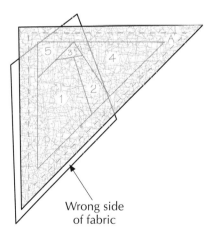

Wrong side of fabric

4. Cut a chunk of fabric or a piece that will cover piece 2 plus ½"-wide seam allowances. Working on the patchwork side, place the fabric over piece 1, with right sides together. Make sure the fabric covers the entire line between pieces 1 and 2 and that it will completely cover piece 2 after it is sewn and flipped. This is like the adding the first strip to a Log Cabin block.

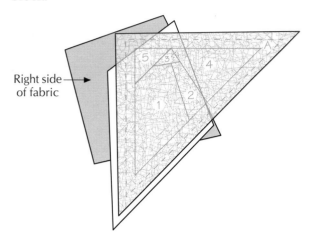

Right side of fabric

TIP

The piece you are adding always should cover the last piece you put down. To check if a piece is in the right place, use the thumb and first finger of both hands to pinch the layers of fabric and interfacing at the ends of the line. Holding the layers, turn them over to check that the fabric covers the line between your fingers.

The art of foundation piecing consists of sewing pieces that, when sewn and flipped, will cover the area you intend them to. It may seem a bit strange at first, but once you get the knack it is easy. Adding the second piece—the first time you must estimate size and position—is always the hardest. Once you get past the second piece, you will get into the swing of it.

5. Turn the foundation over to the traced side. Machine stitch along the line between pieces 1 and 2, starting and stopping 2 stitches beyond each end of the line. Do NOT stitch further; any extra stitches will get in the way when you trim seam allowances later. Trim the thread tails to ¼"; this helps prevent unraveling.

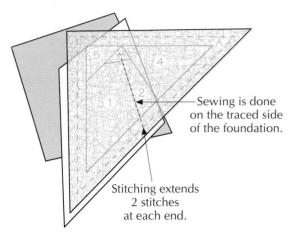

Sewing is done on the traced side of the foundation.

Stitching extends 2 stitches at each end.

If you are hand sewing, do not stitch beyond the line. Knot one end of your thread, then begin sewing ⅛" from the end of the line. Stitch to the end, then reverse direction and stitch along the line to the other end. Reverse again and finish with a couple of backstitches ⅛" from the end of the line.

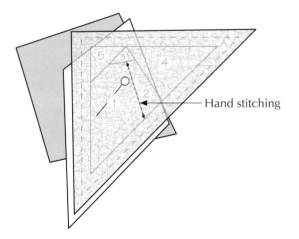

Hand stitching

6. Working from the traced side, fold back the interfacing and trim the seam allowance of the edges just sewn to ⅛". It is important to trim the seam allowance immediately after sewing the seam. Be careful to turn back the interfacing so you do not trim it as well.

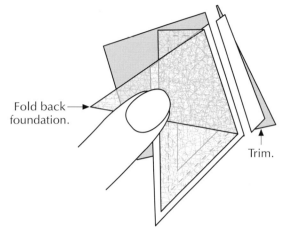

Fold back foundation.

Trim.

7. Turn the foundation to the patchwork side, flip piece 2 over, and press. Trim excess fabric around piece 2, leaving a generous ½"-wide seam allowance. Resist the temptation to trim more closely! If you are hand stitching and are not near an iron, press the seam firmly with your fingernail.

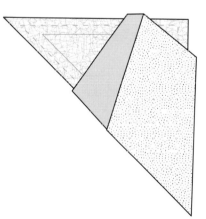

8. Continue in this manner, following the piecing order, until the section is complete. Remember to leave generous ½"-wide seam allowances around the edge of the section.

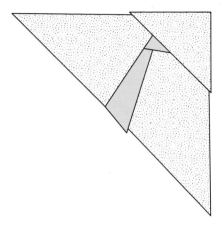

9. Complete all sections of the block in the same manner, adding pieces in order.
10. Lay out the block so that each section is placed correctly. Refer to "Joining Sections" for each block.
11. With a rotary cutter and ruler, trim the section edges you are about to sew. Trim ¼" from the line marking the edge of the block. Do not trim the other edges yet! If you are hand sewing, use scissors to trim the edges.

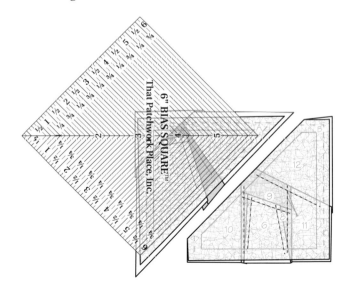

12. Place the sections right sides together. Line up the two sections by pushing a pin through at the corners or at the match points. You do not need to pin the sections together; pushing the pin through both pieces and matching the cut edges will align them correctly.

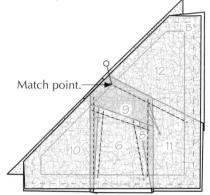

Match point.

13. Once the two pieces are aligned, hold them tightly together by pinching them between the fingers of your left hand. Remove the pin and immediately go to the sewing machine. Stitch the pieces together, stitching from cut edge to cut edge along the traced line of the top section. *Press this seam open.* Spritzing the seam with water will help it lie flat.

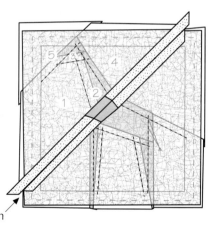

Press seam open.

For hand sewing, continue to sew along the marked lines. Do not sew into the seam allowances. Press the seam flat with your fingernail, pressing the seam allowances open.

14. Continue in this manner until the block is complete. Press well.

15. At last you can trim the outside of the block! Before you begin, there are some points to consider. As already noted, these blocks may be slightly inaccurate, so compensate for this when you trim. Note where the edges of the animal design are in relationship to the edges of the block; trim carefully to avoid trimming part of the animal. There are three kinds of blocks, requiring three different treatments:

- If the background almost completely surrounds the animal (or the animal design touches the edge with a triangular point or points), trim any two adjacent edges ¼" from the traced line (the line indicating the block edge). Then, measure from these cut edges and trim to make the block 4½" x 4½". These are mostly birds, such as the hummingbird on page 74.
- If a straight edge of the animal forms one or more edges of the block, such as the Dolphin block on page 62 or the Donkey block on page 63, trim ¼" from the edge of the animal. Then, trim the background sides (or sides with triangular points), adjusting to the size required. For example, for the Dolphin block, begin by trimming the edge with the dolphin's nose.
- If a straight edge of the animal forms the edge of the block on two opposite sides or on three sides, you will likely add background strips. These blocks do not have two adjacent edges of background to trim. Trim the block ¼" outside the traced line. Cut background strips an extra ¼" wide, then add the strips as described below.

ADDING BACKGROUND STRIPS AND BORDERS

For some blocks, such as the Black Bear on page 51, you will need to add background strips to make the finished block 4" square. The strip measurements for these blocks include an extra ¼" to help compensate for inaccuracies (so the seam allowance is calculated at ¾" rather than the usual ½"). After finishing, trim the block to the exact size required.

The most accurate way to add borders to these small and sometimes uneven blocks is to cut generous strips, adding an extra ¼" to the required width. Stitch the strips to the block, then trim to the desired size. *The block instructions include strip measurements that increase each block to 5" x 5", finished size.*

To eliminate unnecessary strips, combine the measurements for background and border strips (including the extra ¼"). For example, the Flamingo block on page 68 has a 1" strip on one side, so to make the block 5" x 5", finished size, add a 2¼" strip to this side (instead of the 1" strip) and 1¼" strips to the other three sides.

ADDING DETAILS

Details such as eyes, ears, and tails bring these designs to life. You can appliqué or embroider these details, or use small buttons and beads.

Using Fusible Web for Appliqué

The tiny details in these blocks are not really suitable for traditional appliqué (where you turn a seam allowance under). Instead, apply small details with fusible web, then use a few machine or hand stitches to secure the shapes.

1. Cut out a small piece of paper-backed fusible web. Using a pencil, draw or trace the desired shape on the paper side of the web. *Note:* Remember to *reverse* the final shape for fusing.
2. Place the fusible web, nubby side down, on your fabric. Following the manufacturer's instructions, press the fusible web on the fabric.
3. Cut out the shape, peel away the paper, then position the shape on your block. Press.
4. Using a running stitch or buttonhole stitch (page 12), stitch the shape in place.

Making Tails

Some of the animal designs, such as the Cat, Tiger, and Lion blocks, include long, thin tails. Make these using one of the following methods.

FABRIC TUBE

This method works especially well for the Cat block. I recommend cutting the fabric on the bias if possible, but you may have to cut on the straight of grain for a striped tail.

1. Cut a strip of fabric that is twice the finished width, plus ½" for seam allowances. For example, for a ⅜"-wide tail (finished size), cut a 1¼"-wide strip.

2. Fold the strip in half lengthwise, right sides together, and stitch the long edge. Stitch a curve at one end of the fabric tube as shown.

Fold

Stitch. →

3. Trim the seam allowance to a scant ⅛". Using a loop turner or safety pin, turn the tube right side out. Referring to the block pattern, trim the tail to the desired length.

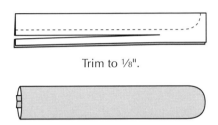

Trim to ⅛".

4. Insert the tail into a seam before sewing or fold in the seam allowances at the cut end, then hand stitch the tail to the block.

FOLDED STRIP

This method works well for the Tiger and Leopard blocks.

1. Working on the bias, if possible, cut a strip of fabric that is 3 times the finished width. For example, for a ¼"-wide tail (finished size), cut a ¾"-wide strip.
2. Trim one end of the strip in a V shape.
3. Working on the long sides, finger-press (do not use an iron) the strip into thirds. Hand baste down the center, folding the sides under as shown.

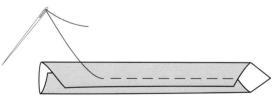

Fold and baste.

4. Shape the strip into a curve and press well, spritzing with water as needed. Referring to the block pattern for placement, hand stitch the strip to the block. Neaten the end by trimming and folding in the seam allowance.

 ←— Neaten end.

PLAITED FLOSS

Here is a fun and easy way to make a tail like that in the Elephant block on page 66 or the Zebra block on page 101.

1. Thread your needle with 6 strands of embroidery floss, each approximately 9" long.
2. From the right side of the finished block, take a small stitch where you want the base of the tail.

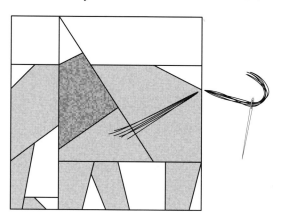

3. Pull the floss until it is even on both sides of the stitch, so you have 12 strands. Remove the needle.
4. Divide the strands into 3 groups of 4.
5. Plait the 3 groups to the desired length, then tie a knot and trim as shown.

Embroidery

Use simple embroidery stitches to make eyes, legs, and other details. Refer to the block patterns for the color and number of strands you will need.

BACKSTITCH

The backstitch is ideal for lettering.

BUTTONHOLE STITCH

Use the buttonhole stitch for manes, or to enhance and outline appliqués.

Right-handed buttonhole stitch

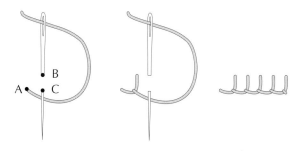

Left-handed buttonhole stitch

CHAIN STITCH

This is probably my favorite stitch because it makes a strong line and is invaluable for filling small shapes. I also use a stitch that I call a "double chain," which is simply a chain stitch inside another chain stitch. This last is especially good for making ears.

Right-handed chain stitch

Left-handed chain stitch

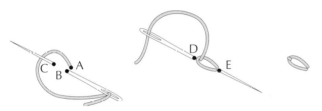

Detached chain or lazy daisy stitch

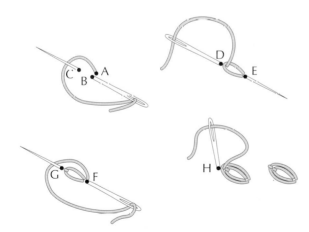

Double chain stitch

Here is an easy way to make eyes using a chain stitch.

1. Thread your needle with 2 strands of embroidery floss.
2. Make a small single chain stitch for the center of the eye. Then, using a small stitch, embroider rings of chain stitches around the center stitch. This technique enables you to change the floss color for the pupils and irises.

For odd shapes, such as ears, stitch the outline of the shape, then fill in the center. *Note:* This is opposite to the way you stitch a circle.

FRENCH KNOT

French knots are useful when you need just a dot, as for tiny eyes.

French knot

STEM STITCH

Use a stem stitch to make smooth lines. I like to sew directly on the line rather than at a slight angle as is sometimes suggested for this stitch.

Stem stitch

STRAIGHT STITCH

Use straight stitches for whiskers, or bunches of straight stitches for eyes and noses. For odd shapes, stitch the outline of the shape, then fill in the center.

Straight stitch

Straight-stitch fill

TURNING YOUR BLOCKS INTO QUILTS

Many books explain the basics of constructing a quilt, so I give only a few critical points. For more information, look at *Go Wild with Quilts, Go Wild with Quilts—Again*, or your favorite basic quilt book.

Assembling the Quilt Top

1. Stitch the block or blocks, following the foundation piecing directions on pages 6–7. Remember to trim the sides with the design first, then trim the background—adjusting for any inaccuracies.

2. Add strips of background fabric to make the block the desired size (see page 10).

3. Add details such as eyes, ears, noses, and tails, following the instructions on page 11.

4. Cut shapes and/or piece traditional blocks as desired to make the quilt center.

5. Assemble the quilt top as shown. In general, you will sew blocks into rows, then join the rows.

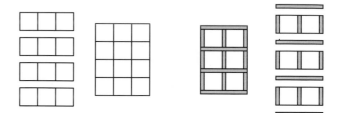

Cutting Size for Squares, Rectangles, and Triangles

Use the following magic numbers to determine the desired cutting size:

- Add ½" to the finished size of squares, rectangles, and strips.

Finished size + ½"

- Add ⅞" to the finished size of a square that will be cut on the diagonal to make two half-square triangles.

Finished size + ⅞"

- Add 1¼" to the finished size of a square that will be cut twice diagonally to make four quarter-square triangles.

Finished size + 1¼"

An Accurate ¼"-Wide Seam Allowance

When sewing, ensure an accurate seam allowance in one of the following ways:

- Use a specially designed ¼" foot made for your sewing machine.
- Set the needle position so there is exactly ¼" between the needle and the edge of the foot. (I keep a little bit of template plastic with a ¼" grid handy; it's a great help for checking my seam allowance.)
- Measure ¼" from the needle. Place a strip of masking tape (or other suitable tape) on the machine to mark the ¼". Use the tape as a guide when you sew.

Adding Borders

Borders may have straight or mitered corners. Always measure through the center of the quilt.

STRAIGHT-CUT CORNERS

1. Measure the length of the quilt top at the center, from raw edge to raw edge. Cut 2 border strips to that measurement. Join the border strips to the sides, matching ends.
2. Measure the width of the quilt top at the center from raw edge to raw edge, including the border pieces just added. Cut 2 border strips to that measurement. Join border strips to the top and bottom of the quilt, matching ends.

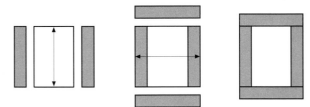

For a variation on the straight-cut border, add corner squares.

1. Measure the length of the quilt top at the center, from raw edge to raw edge. Cut 2 border strips to that measurement.
2. Measure the width of the quilt top at the center, from raw edge to raw edge. Cut 2 border strips to that measurement.
3. Cut corner squares the same width as the borders, including seam allowances. For example, if the border strips are 2" wide, cut 2" x 2" corner squares.
4. Join the corner squares to the border strips and the borders strips to the quilt top as shown.

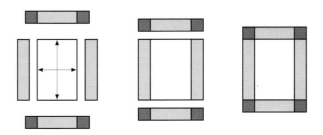

MITERED CORNERS

1. Estimate the finished outside dimensions of your quilt, including borders. Cut 4 border strips to that length, plus 2" to 3".
2. Using pins, mark the ¼" seam intersections on all four corners of the quilt top. Mark the center of each side.

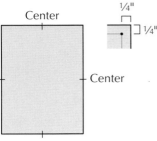

3. On the border strips, use pins to mark the center of each side and ¼" in from where the corner of the quilt will be.

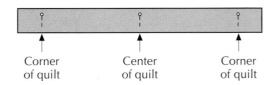

4. With right sides together, lay a border strip on the quilt top as shown, matching center and corner marks. Stitch from corner mark to corner mark and no further. Open out. Repeat for remaining border strips. The stitching lines must meet exactly at the corners.

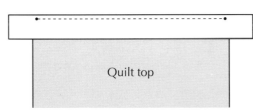

5. With right sides together, fold the quilt diagonally so that the border strips are aligned. Using a right-angle or quilter's ruler marked with a 45° angle, draw a line on the wrong side of the border strip, from the corner mark to the outside edge as shown.

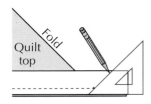

6. Secure the borders with pins and stitch on the drawn line. Open out the top and make sure the seam is flat and accurate before trimming the seam allowances. Press the seam open. Repeat for the remaining corners.

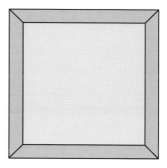

Quilting

Machine quilting is ideal for these small blocks. It is possible to hand quilt, but the extra thicknesses of seam allowances and foundation make it a little more difficult. If you are making single-block quilts, you will not need much quilting.

For a softer, hand-quilted appearance, use clear monofilament thread. (I like this thread because it blends into all colors.) Use the monofilament thread on the top of the machine only, and a regular thread to match the quilt backing in the bobbin.

Layer the quilt top, batting, and backing, then hand or pin baste. Quilt as desired, then use a rotary cutter to trim the sides and corners straight and even before binding. For more information on marking, layering, and quilting, look at *Go Wild with Quilts, Go Wild with Quilts—Again,* or your favorite basic quilting book.

Binding

I prefer to attach binding as described for borders rather than as a single length around the quilt, which can cause wavy edges. For a large quilt, cut binding strips 2" wide; for a small quilt or block, cut binding strips 1¾" wide.

1. Measure the length of the quilt sandwich through the center and cut binding strips to that measurement, piecing as necessary. Fold each strip in half lengthwise, right side out, and press for double-fold binding.
2. Pin the binding strips to the side edges. Stitch in place.
3. Fold and finger-press the side bindings over to the back of the quilt and pin in place.

Back of quilt | Binding folded over and pinned

4. Measure the width of the quilt sandwich through the center, then cut binding strips to that measurement plus 1", piecing as necessary. Fold each strip in half lengthwise, right side out, and press.
5. Pin the binding strips to the top and bottom edges. Stitch in place.
6. Fold and finger-press the top and bottom bindings over to the back of the quilt and pin in place. Blindstitch all four bindings in place, trimming and folding corner edges neatly.

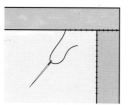

Ark Quilt
41" x 51"

Owl

14" x 14"

Cat
11¾" x 11¾"

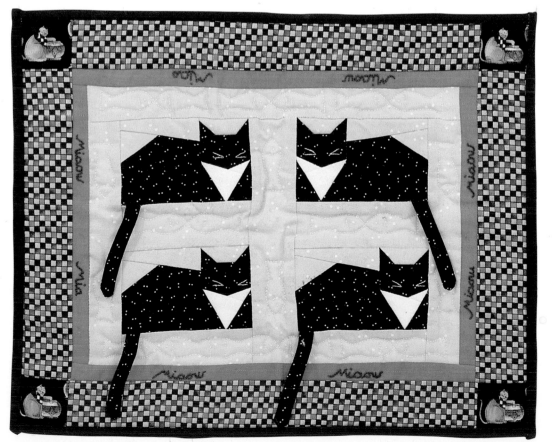

Miaow Cats
12¼" x 15¼"
by Beth McConchie

Pig
6" x 6⅛"
by Dianne Firth

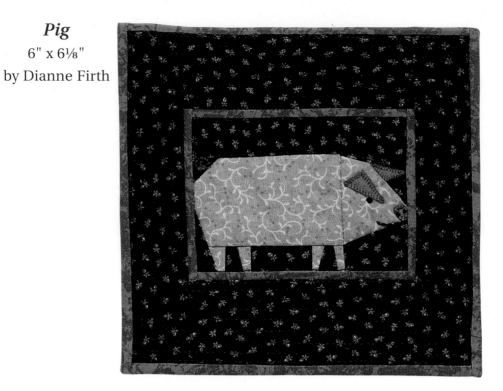

Rabbit
9" x 9"

Goat
6" x 6"
by Carolyn Daniel

Donkey
7" x 7"
by Becky Peters

Duck
7" x 7"
by Anne Eccleston

I Never Saw a Purple Cow
7" x 7"

Toucan
10¾" x 10¾"

Share the Earth
9" x 9"

Koala
7" x 7"
by Beryl Jeeves

Panda
6½" x 6½"

Butterfly Ninepatch
21" x 21"

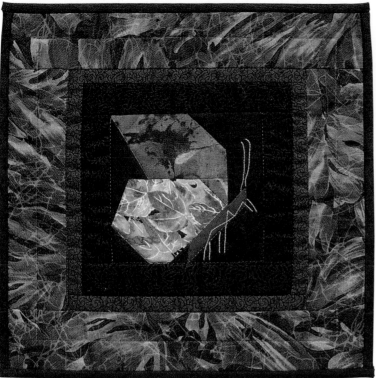

Butterfly
9¼" x 9¼"
by Betty Hand

Peacock
7½" x 7½"

Peacock
10" x 10"

Loon
8" x 8"

Beaver
10" x 10"
by Anieta Barendrecht

Buffalo
16" x 16"

Dolphin
22" x 22"

Blue Jay
8" x 8"

Pelican
8" x 8"

Hummingbird
7" x 7"

Flamingo
8½" x 8½"

Hummingbird
18" x 18"

Turkey
7½" x 7½"

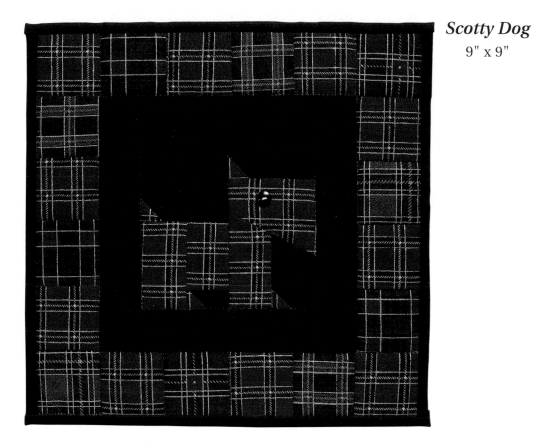

Scotty Dog
9" x 9"

Cardinal
6½" x 6½"

Bald Eagle
7" x 7"

Parrot
(Crimson Rosella)
8½" x 8½"

Beaver

9" x 9"

Hen
7¼" x 7¼"
by Iris Hockley

Rooster
7¼" x 7¼"
by Iris Hockley

***A Woman's Work
is Never Done***

9½" x 9½"

Rooster

10" x 10"

Penguin Quilt

9¾" x 11½"

by Ann-Maree Jacobs

Penguin Beach
8½" x 9¾"
by Beth Miller

Puffin
8½" x 8½"

Puffin
5" x 5"
by Elaine Niit

Elephant
9" x 9"

Elephant
6¾" x 6¾"
by Robyn Oats

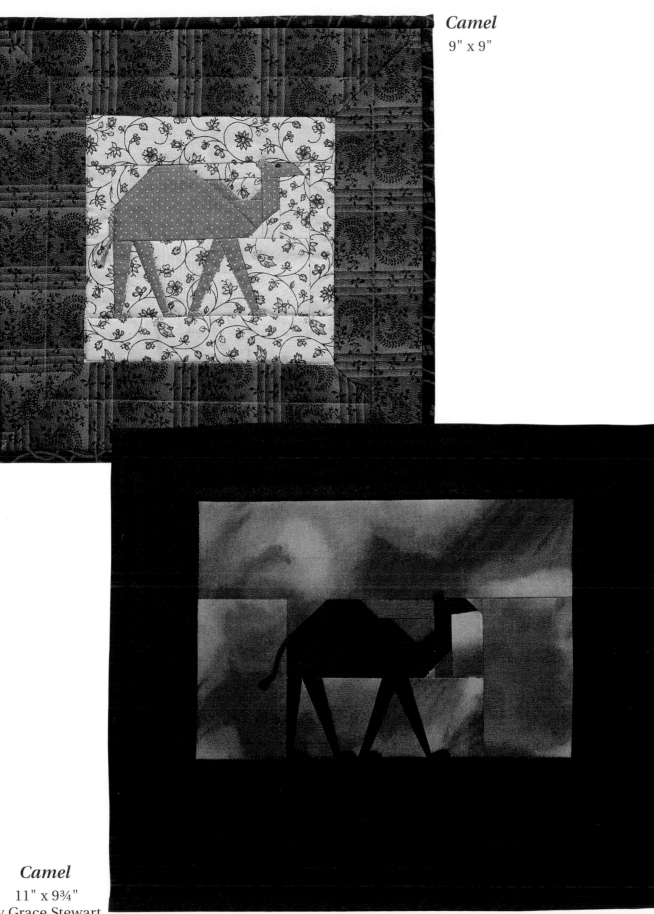

Camel
9" x 9"

Camel
11" x 9¾"
by Grace Stewart

Farm Quilt

26" x 26"

Bear in the Woods
28" x 28"

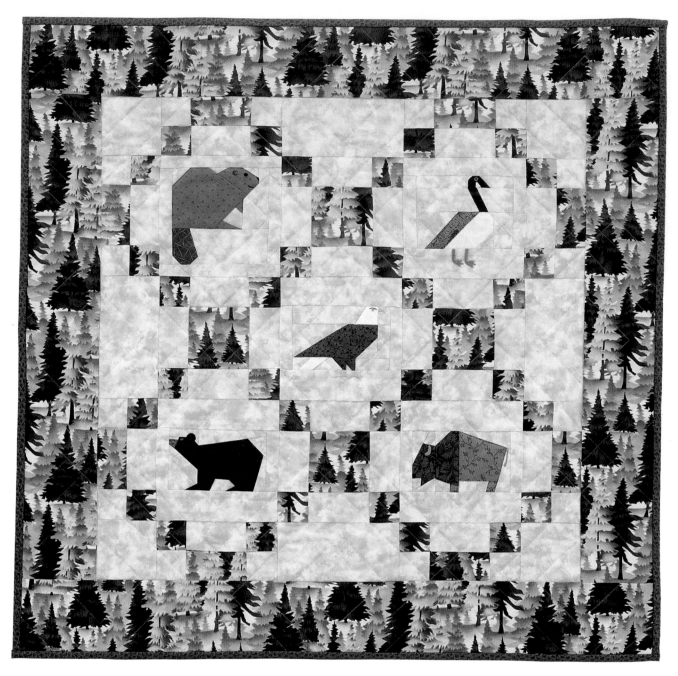

North American Animals Quilt

26" x 26"

Australian Animals Quilt
21½" x 28½"

Zoo Quilt
17¼" x 17¼"

Jumpin' Jumbos
30" x 30"

Bald Eagle

COLORS

Head and tail—white
Body and legs—dark brown
Background fabric

JOINING SECTIONS

A + B + C

SIZE OPTIONS

Finished size: 4" x 4"

For a 5" x 5" finished size, add 1¼"-wide strips, then trim the block to 5½" x 5½".

ADDING DETAILS

Eye center—single chain stitch with 2 strands of black floss

Brow—stem stitch with 1 strand of black floss

Outer eye—chain stitch around eye center with 1 strand of yellow floss

Beak and feet—chain stitch with 2 strands of yellow floss

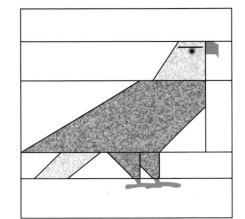

SEE COLOR PHOTOS
ON PAGES 36 AND 46

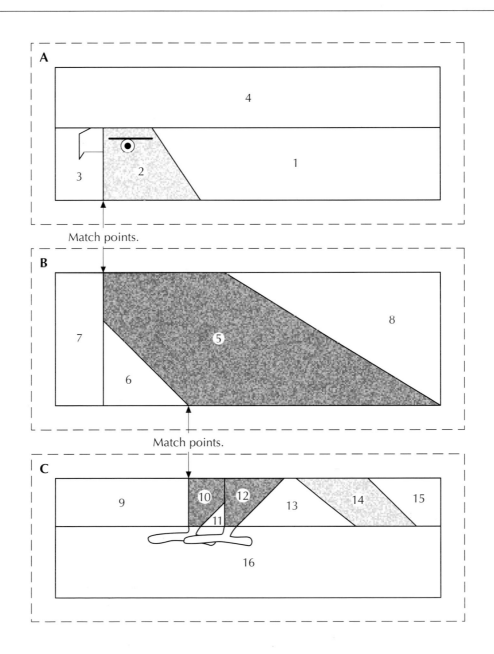

A

4

3   2   1

Match points.

B

7   6   5   8

Match points.

C

9   10   12   13   14   15

11

16

Beaver

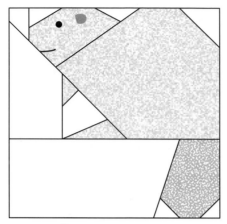

SEE COLOR PHOTOS
ON PAGES 28, 37, AND 46

COLORS

Body—brown
Tail—dark brown
Background fabric

JOINING SECTIONS

1. A + B
2. (A-B) + C

SIZE OPTIONS

Finished size: 4" x 4"

For a 5" x 5" finished size, add
1¼"-wide strips, then trim the block
to 5½" x 5½".

ADDING DETAILS

Eye—chain stitch with 2 strands
of black floss
Mouth—stem stitch with 2 strands
of black floss
Ear—chain stitch with 2 strands
of brown floss

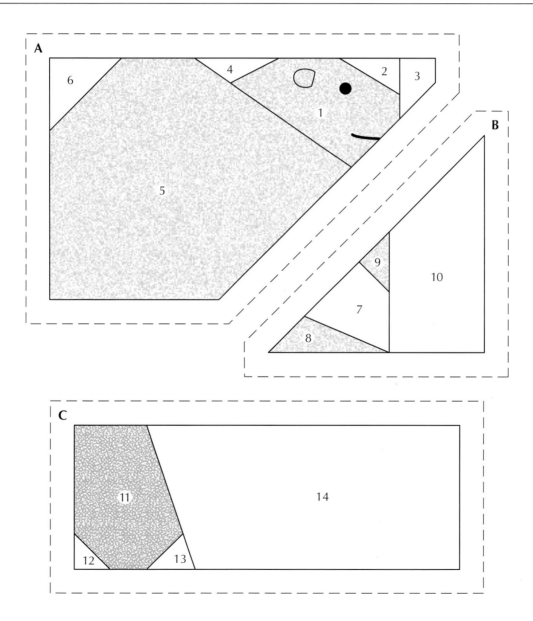

COLORS

Body—black
Nose—brown
Background fabric

JOINING SECTIONS

A + B

SIZE OPTIONS

Finished size: 4" x 2½"

For a 4" x 4" finished size, add 1½"-wide strips to the top and bottom, then trim the block to 4½" x 4½".

For a 5" x 5" finished size, add 1¼"-wide strips to the sides and 2"-wide strips to the top and bottom, then trim the block to 5½" x 5½".

ADDING DETAILS

Eye center—chain stitch with 2 strands of black floss

Outer eye—chain stitch with 2 strands of light brown floss

Ear—appliqué using black fabric (see page 11)

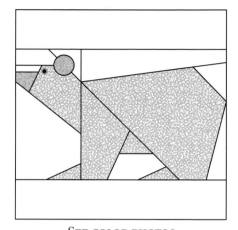

SEE COLOR PHOTOS
ON PAGES 45 AND 46

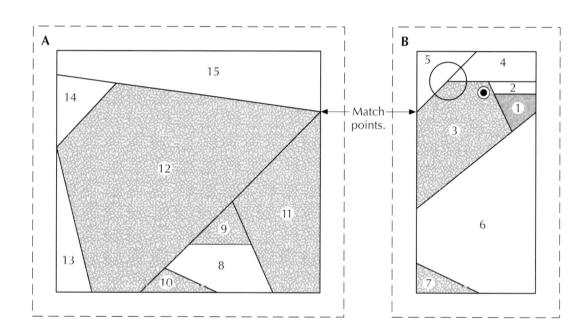

← Match points. →

Blue Jay

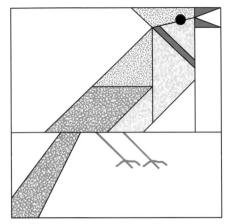

SEE COLOR PHOTO ON PAGE 31

COLORS

Crest and upper wing (Pieces 3 and 6)—blue

Necklace and beak (Pieces 2, 11, and 13)—black

Face and breast (Pieces 1, 5, and 7)—white

Lower wing and tail (Pieces 4 and 15)—blue-and-black print

Background fabric

JOINING SECTIONS

1. A + B
2. (A-B) + C
3. (A-C) + D

SIZE OPTIONS

Finished size: 4" x 4"

For a 5" x 5" finished size, add 1¼"-wide strips, then trim the block to 5½" x 5½".

ADDING DETAILS

Eye—chain stitch with 2 strands of black floss

Legs—chain stitch with 2 strands of gray floss

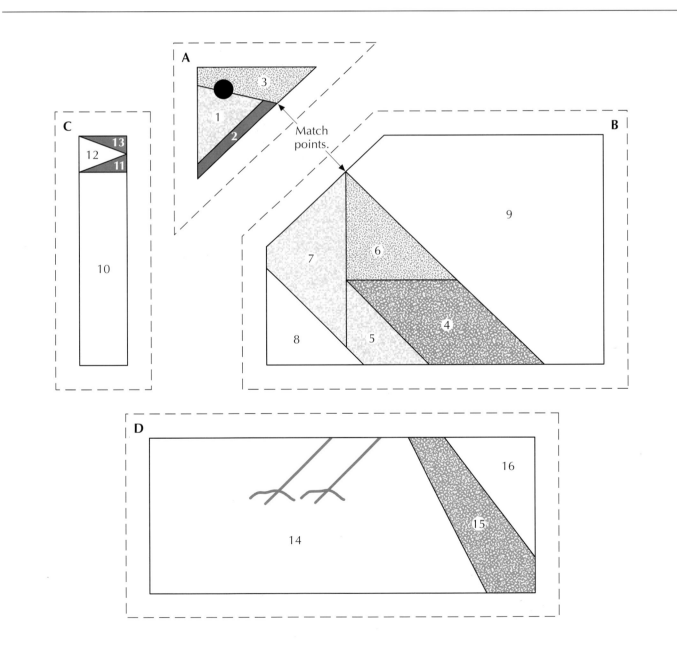

Buffalo (Bison)

COLORS

Head and shoulders—dark brown
Body and legs—brown
Background fabric

JOINING SECTIONS

A + B + C

SIZE OPTIONS

Finished size: 4" x 2½"

For a 4" x 4" finished size, add 1½"-wide strips to the top and bottom, then trim the block to 4½" x 4½".

For a 5" x 5" finished size, add 1¼"-wide strips to the sides and 2"-wide strips to the top and bottom, then trim the block to 5½" x 5½".

ADDING DETAILS

Tail—chain stitch with 2 strands of dark brown floss

Tassel on tail—straight stitch with 2 strands of dark brown floss

Eye—double chain stitch with 2 strands of black floss

Nose—straight stitch with 2 strands of black floss

Horn—chain stitch with 2 strands of light brown floss

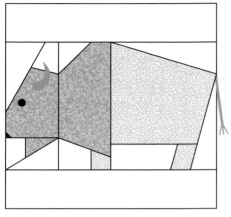

SEE COLOR PHOTOS
ON PAGES 29 AND 46

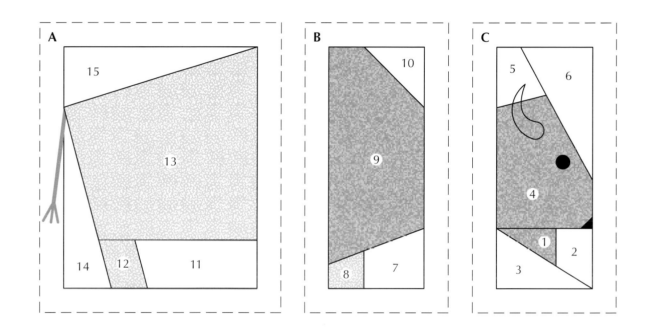

Butterfly

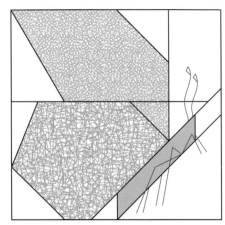

SEE COLOR PHOTOS
ON PAGES 26 AND 27

COLORS

Butterflies come in many colors;
choose your favorites.

Upper wing (Pieces 1 and 8)

Lower wing (Piece 5)

Body (Piece 10)

Background fabric

JOINING SECTIONS

1. A + B
2. (A-B) + C

SIZE OPTIONS

Finished size: 4" x 4"

For a 5" x 5" finished size, add
1¼"-wide strips, then trim the block
to 5½" x 5½".

ADDING DETAILS

Feelers—stem stitch with 1 strand
of black or contrasting color of floss

Legs (optional)—stem stitch with
1 strand of black or contrasting
color of floss

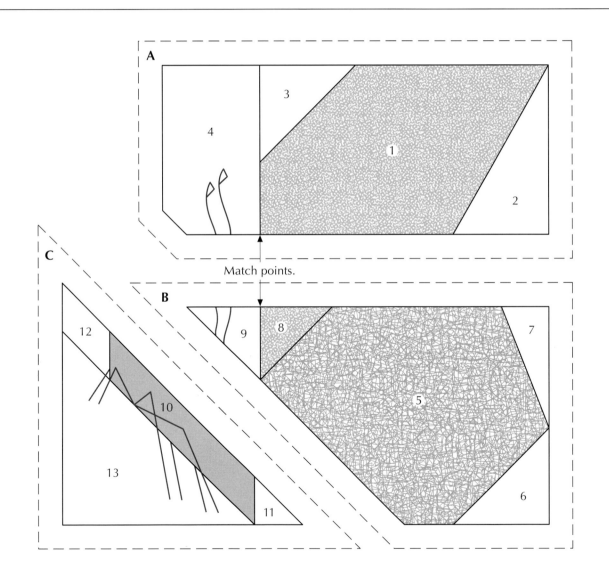

Match points.

Camel

COLORS

Body—light brown
Background fabric

JOINING SECTIONS

1. A + B
2. (A-B) + C

SIZE OPTIONS

Finished size: 4" x 3¼"

For a 4" x 4" finished size,
add a 1½"-wide strip to the top,
then trim the block to 4½" x 4½".

For a 5" x 5" finished size, add
1¼"-wide strips to the sides and
bottom and a 2"-wide strip to the top,
then trim the block to 5½" x 5½".

ADDING DETAILS

Eye—double chain stitch with
2 strands of black floss

Tail—plait with 12 strands of light
brown floss (see page 12)

Ear and feet—chain stitch with
2 strands of light brown floss

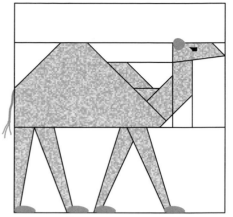

SEE COLOR PHOTOS
ON PAGES 17 AND 43

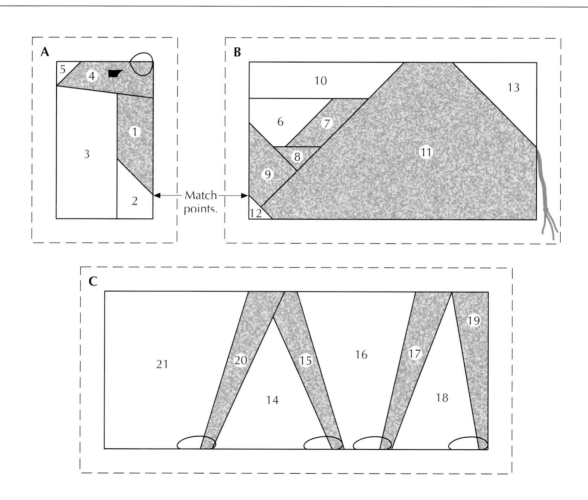

Canada Goose

SEE COLOR PHOTO ON PAGE 46

COLORS

Head and neck—black
Breast—light gray
Wing—brown
Background fabric

JOINING SECTIONS

A + B + C

SIZE OPTIONS

Finished size: 4" x 4"

For a 5" x 5" finished size, add
1¼"-wide strips, then trim the block
to 5½" x 5½".

ADDING DETAILS

Eye—chain stitch with 2 strands
of black floss

Circle around eye—stem stitch with
1 strand of gray floss

Legs—chain stitch with 2 strands
of gray floss

Cheek patch—straight stitch with
2 strands of white floss

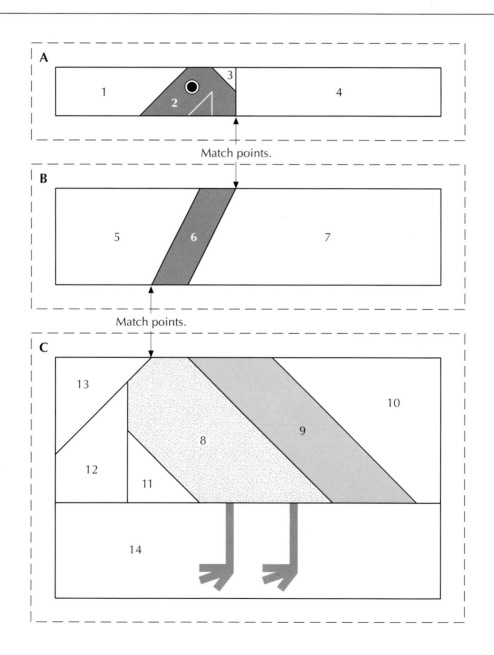

Cardinal

COLORS

Body—red
Face patch—black
Background fabric

JOINING SECTIONS

A + B

SIZE OPTIONS

Finished size: 4" x 4"

For a 5" x 5" finished size, add
1¼"-wide strips, then trim the block
to 5½" x 5½".

ADDING DETAILS

Eye—chain stitch with 2 strands
of black floss
Legs—chain stitch with 2 strands
of black floss
Beak—straight stitch with 2 strands
of red floss
Circle around eye—stem stitch with
1 strand of red floss

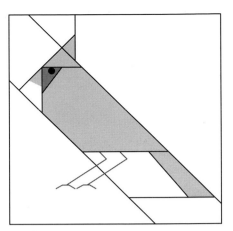

SEE COLOR PHOTO ON PAGE 35

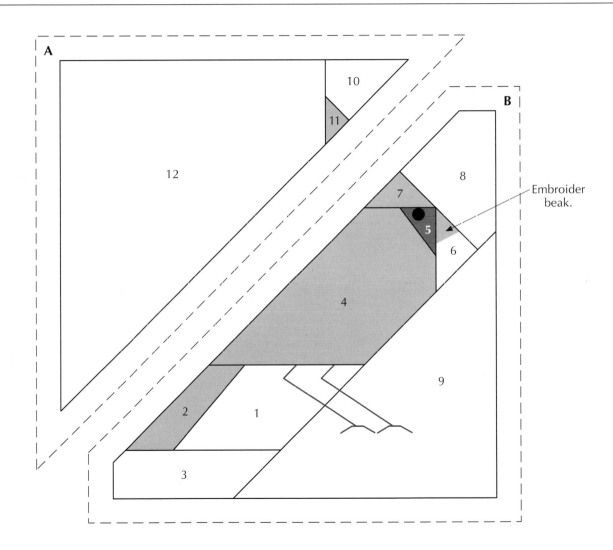

Embroider beak.

Cat

See color photos
on page 19

COLORS

Head and body—any cat color, such as black, orange, or gray

Chest—color that contrasts with head and body

Background fabric

JOINING SECTIONS

A + B

SIZE OPTIONS

Finished size: 4" x 2½"

For a 4" x 4" finished size, add a 2¼"-wide strip to the bottom, then trim the block to 4½" x 4½".

For a 5" x 5" finished size, add 1¼"-wide strips to the sides and top and a 2¾"-wide strip to the bottom, then trim the block to 5½" x 5½".

ADDING DETAILS

Eyes and mouth—stem stitch with 2 strands of black or a contrasting color of floss

Nose—straight stitch with 2 strands of black or a contrasting color of floss

Whiskers—stem stitch with 1 strand of white or a contrasting color of floss

Back leg curve and feet—stem stitch with 1 strand of floss a shade darker (or lighter) than cat body

Tail—make a fabric tube, ⅜" x 3½" finished size (see page 11); stitch into seam when adding strip below cat

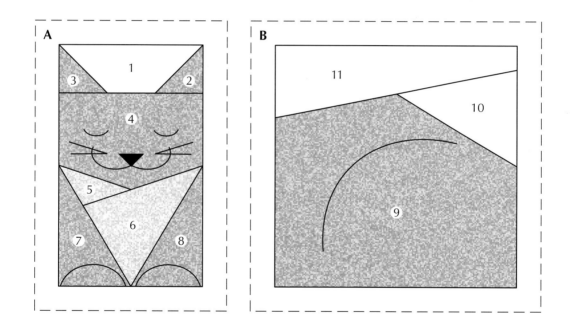

COLORS

Body—yellow

SIZE OPTIONS

Finished size: ¾" x ¾"

For a 1¾" x 1¾" finished size, add 1¼"-wide strips, then trim the block to 2¼" x 2¼".

ADDING DETAILS

Eye—French knot with 2 strands of black floss

Beak and legs—straight stitch with 2 strands of orange floss

NOTE: You can reverse and rotate this block. Remember to change the position of the legs and feet.

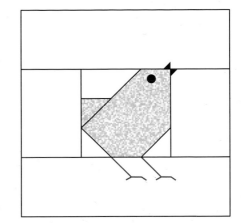

SEE COLOR PHOTO ON PAGE 39

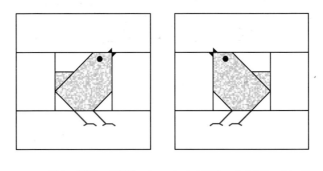

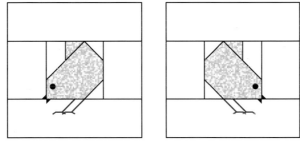

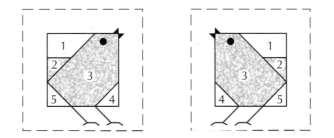

Cow

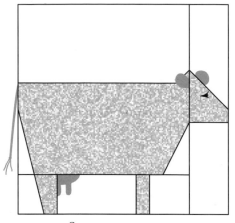

SEE COLOR PHOTOS
ON PAGES 22 AND 44

COLORS

Body—black-and-white print or light brown

Background fabric

JOINING SECTIONS

1. A + B
2. (A-B) + C

SIZE OPTIONS

Finished size: 4" x 4"

For a 5" x 5" finished size, add 1¼ "-wide strips, then trim the block to 5½" x 5½".

ADDING DETAILS

Ear—chain stitch with 2 strands of floss in a matching color

Tail—plait with 12 strands of floss in a matching color (see page 12)

Eye—double chain stitch with 2 strands of black floss

Udder—chain stitch with 2 strands of pink floss

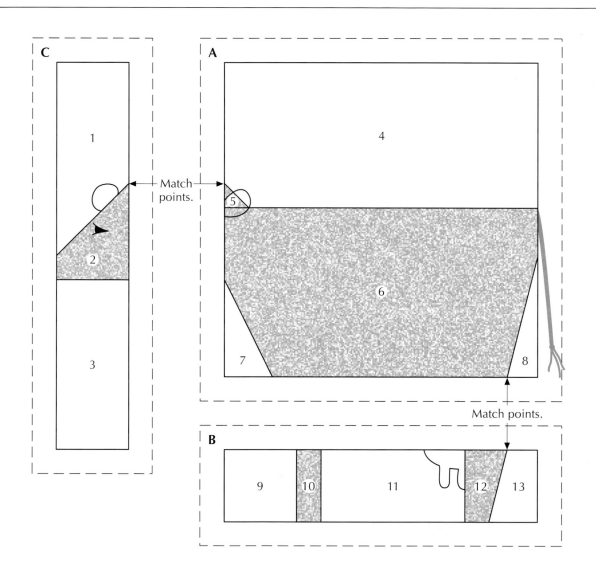

Dog

COLORS
Dog—black-and-white print
or brown
Background fabric

JOINING SECTIONS
1. A + B + C
2. (A-C) + D

SIZE OPTIONS
Finished size: 4" x 4"

For a 5" x 5" finished size,
add 1¼"-wide strips, then trim
the block to 5½" x 5½".

ADDING DETAILS
Eye—double chain stitch with
2 strands of black floss

Nose—straight stitch with 2 strands
of black floss

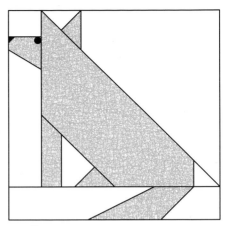

SEE COLOR PHOTO ON PAGE 44

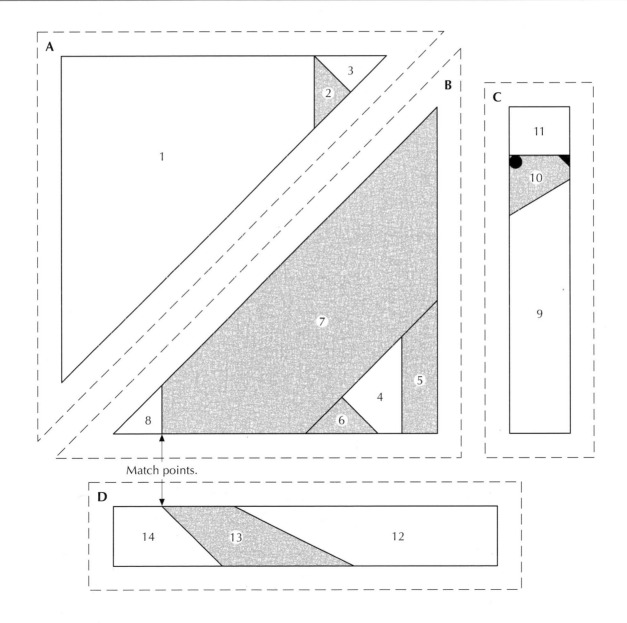

Dolphin

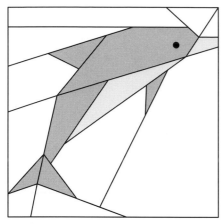

SEE COLOR PHOTO ON PAGE 30

COLORS

Upper body, fins, and tail—dark gray
Belly and nose—light gray
Background fabric

JOINING SECTIONS

1. A + B
2. C + D
3. (A-B) + (C-D)

SIZE OPTIONS

Finished size: 4" x 4"

For a 5" x 5" finished size, add
1¼"-wide strips, then trim the block
to 5½" x 5½".

ADDING DETAILS

Eye—chain stitch with 2 strands
of black floss

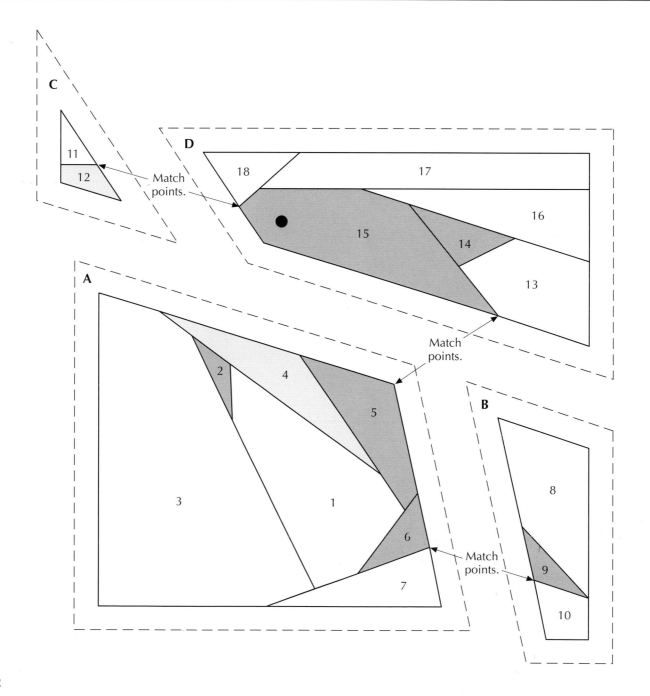

COLORS

Donkey—light brown or light gray
Background fabric

JOINING SECTIONS

1. A + B
2. C + D
3. (A-B) + (C-D)
4. (A-D) + E

SIZE OPTIONS

Finished size: 4" x 4"

For a 5" x 5" finished size,
add 1¼"-wide strips, then trim
the block to 5½" x 5½".

ADDING DETAILS

Mane—buttonhole stitch
with 2 strands of dark brown
or dark gray floss

Tail—plait with 12 strands
of floss in a matching color
(see page 12)

Eye—double chain stitch with
2 strands of black floss

Nostril—single chain stitch
with 2 strands of black floss

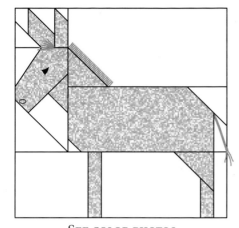

SEE COLOR PHOTOS
ON PAGES 21 AND 44

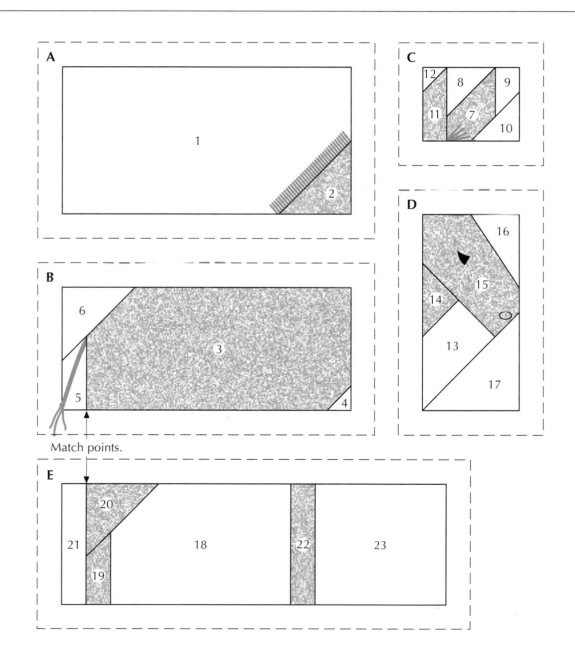

Match points.

Duck

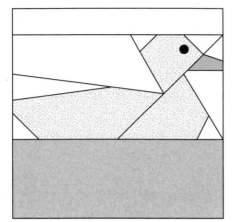

SEE COLOR PHOTOS
ON PAGES 22 AND 44

COLORS
Body—white
Bill—dark yellow
Water—blue
Background fabric

JOINING SECTIONS
1. A + B
2. (A-B) + C

SIZE OPTIONS
Finished size: 4" x 2"

For a 4" x 4" finished size,
add a 1¼"-wide strip to the top
and a 2¼"-wide blue strip
to the bottom, then trim the block
to 4½" x 4½".

For a 5" x 5" finished size, add
1¼"-wide strips to the sides,
a 1¾"-wide strip to the top, and
a 2¾"-wide blue strip to the bottom,
then trim the block to 5½" x 5½".

ADDING DETAILS
Eye—chain stitch with 2 strands
of black floss

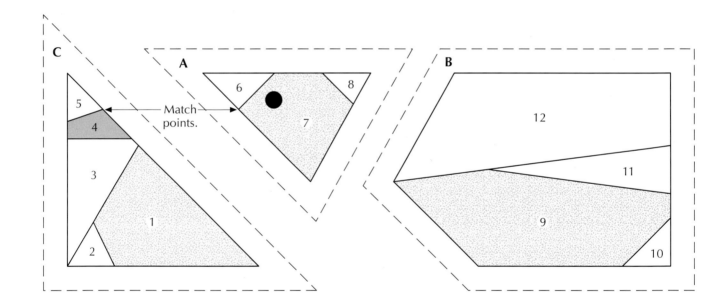

Duckling

COLORS
Body—light yellow
Bill—dark yellow
Background fabric

JOINING SECTIONS
A + B

SIZE OPTIONS
Finished size: 1½" x 1"

For a 2½" x 2½" finished size,
add 1¼"-wide strips to the sides
and 1½"-wide strips to the top
and bottom, then trim the block
to 3" x 3".

ADDING DETAILS
Eye—French knot with 2 strands
of black floss

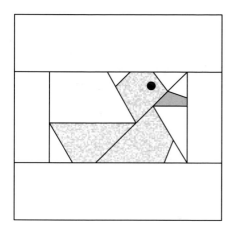

SEE COLOR PHOTO ON PAGE 44

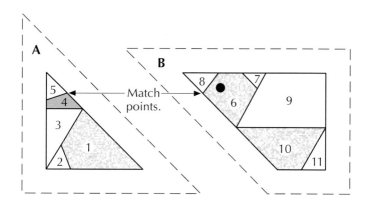

65

Elephant

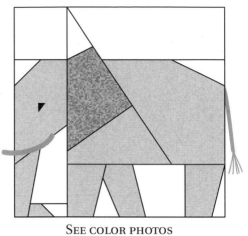

SEE COLOR PHOTOS
ON PAGES 17, 42, AND 48

COLORS

Body and head—light gray
Ear—dark gray or contrasting color
Background fabric

JOINING SECTIONS

1. A + B
2. (A-B) + C
3. (A-C) + D

SIZE OPTIONS

Finished size: 4" x 4"

For a 5" x 5" finished size,
add 1¼"-wide strips, then trim
the block to 5½" x 5½".

ADDING DETAILS

Eye—double chain stitch with
2 strands of black floss

Tusk—chain stitch with 2 strands
of white floss

Tail—plait with 12 strands
of gray floss (see page 12)

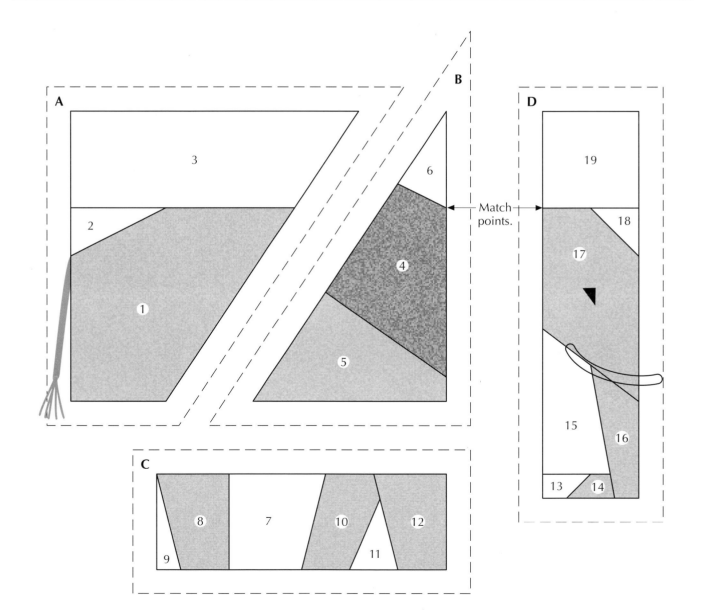

Match points.

Emu

COLORS

Body—brown print
Legs—light brown
Background fabric

JOINING SECTIONS

1. A + B
2. (A-B) + C

SIZE OPTIONS

Finished size: 4" x 4"
For a 5" x 5" finished size, add
1¼"-wide strips, then trim the block
to 5½" x 5½".

ADDING DETAILS

Eye—double chain stitch with
2 strands of black floss

Beak—straight stitch with 2 strands
of dark gray or black floss

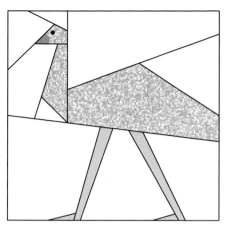

SEE COLOR PHOTO ON PAGE 47

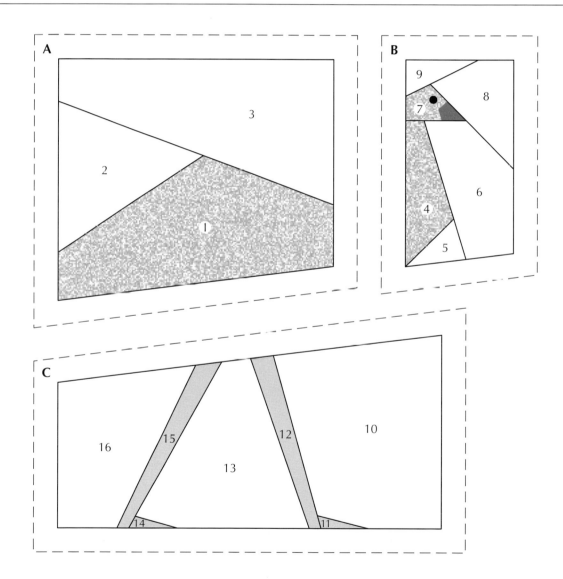

Flamingo

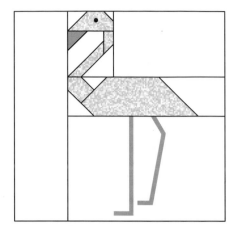

SEE COLOR PHOTOS
ON PAGES 17 AND 32

COLORS

Body—pink
Beak tip—black
Background fabric

JOINING SECTIONS

A + B

SIZE OPTIONS

Finished size: 3" x 4"

For a 4" x 4" finished size,
add a 1¾"-wide strip to the left side,
then trim the block to 4½" x 4½".

For a 5" x 5" finished size,
add a 2¼"-wide strip to the left side
and 1¼"-wide strips to the right side,
top, and bottom, then trim the block
to 5½" x 5½".

ADDING DETAILS

Eye—French knot with 2 strands
of black floss
Legs—chain stitch with 2 strands
of pink floss

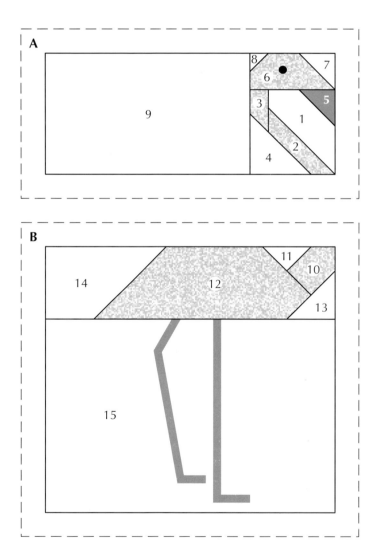

Giraffe

COLORS

Body—dark gold print
Background fabric

JOINING SECTIONS

A + B

SIZE OPTIONS

Finished size: 4" x 4"

For a 5" x 5" finished size, add
1¼"-wide strips, then trim the block
to 5½" x 5½".

ADDING DETAILS

Ear—double chain stitch with
4 strands of dark gold floss

Tail—plait with 12 strands of dark
gold floss (see page 12)

Eye—double chain stitch with
2 strands of black floss

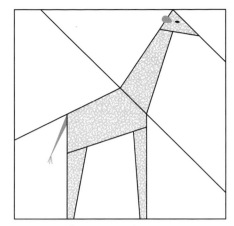

SEE COLOR PHOTOS
ON PAGES 17 AND 48

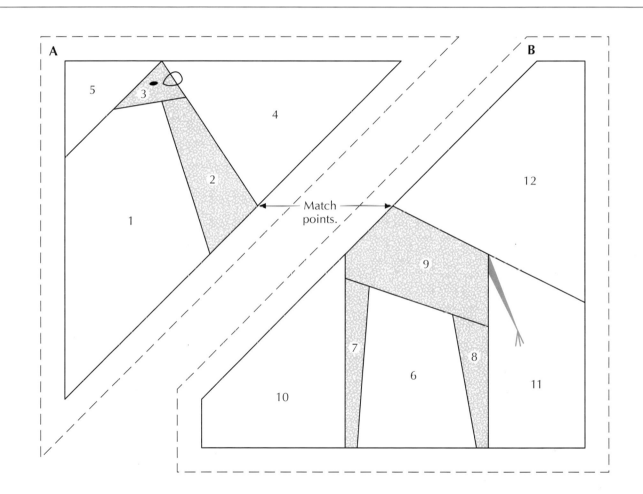

Goat

SEE COLOR PHOTOS
ON PAGES 21 AND 44

COLORS

Goat—cream or light brown
Background fabric

JOINING SECTIONS

1. A + B
2. C + D
3. (A-B) + (C-D)

SIZE OPTIONS

Finished size: 4" x 3"

For a 4" x 4" finished size,
add a 1¾"-wide strip to the top,
then trim the block to 4½" x 4½".

For a 5" x 5" finished size, add
1¼"-wide strips to the sides and
bottom and a 2¼"-wide strip
to the top, then trim the block
to 5½" x 5½".

ADDING DETAILS

Horns—chain stitch with 2 strands
of cream or brown floss

Beard—straight stitch with 2 strands
of cream or brown floss

Eyes—stem stitch with 2 strands
of black floss

Nostrils—single chain stitch with
2 strands of black floss

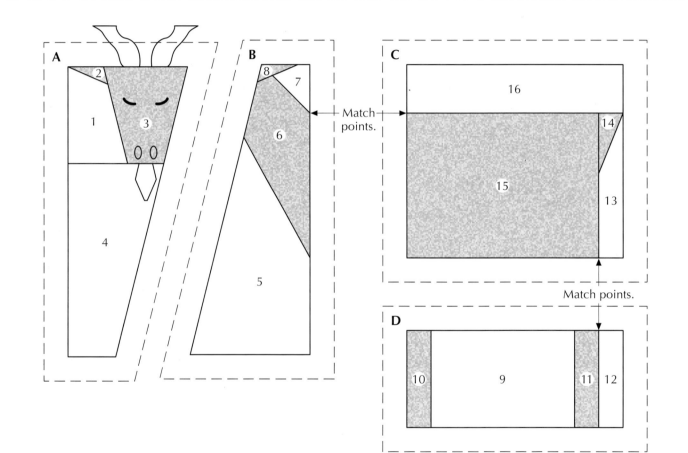

Hen

COLORS

Body—rust, black, or white
Comb and wattle—red
Background fabric

JOINING SECTIONS

A + B

SIZE OPTIONS

Finished size: 4" x 4"

For a 5" x 5" finished size, add 1¼"-wide strips, then trim the block to 5½" x 5½".

ADDING DETAILS

Legs—chain stitch with 2 strands of floss in a matching color

Beak—straight stitch with 2 strands of yellow or a contrasting color of floss

Eye—double chain stitch with 2 strands of black floss

Comb and wattle—appliqué using red fabric (see page 11); buttonhole stitch edges with 1 strand of red floss

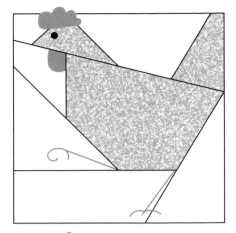

SEE COLOR PHOTOS
ON PAGES 38–39 AND 44

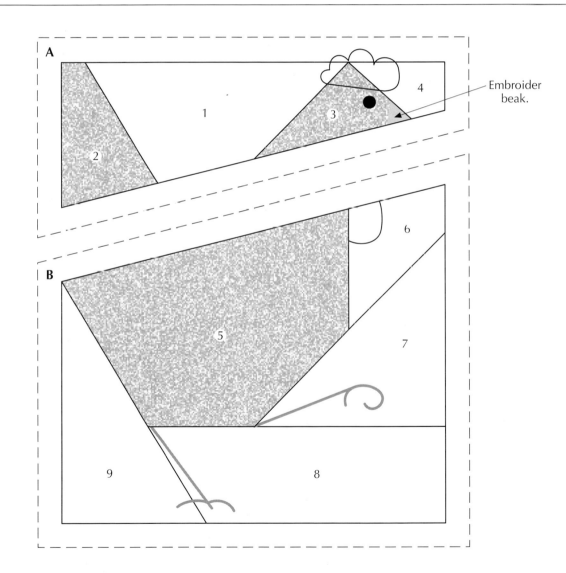

Embroider beak.

Hippopotamus

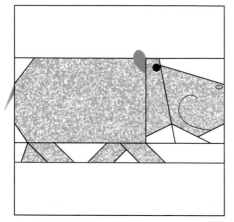

SEE COLOR PHOTO ON PAGE 17

COLORS

Hippopotamus—dark brown
Background fabric

JOINING SECTIONS

1. A + B
2. (A-B) + C

SIZE OPTIONS

Finished size: 4" x 2"

For a 4" x 4" finished size, add
1¾"-wide strips to the top
and bottom, then trim the block
to 4½" x 4½".

For a 5" x 5" finished size, add
1¼"-wide strips to the sides
and 2¼"-wide strips to the top
and bottom, then trim the block
to 5½" x 5½".

ADDING DETAILS

Ear—double chain stitch with
4 strands of dark brown floss

Tail—straight stitch with 4 strands
of dark brown floss after
adding borders

Eye—double chain stitch with
2 strands of black floss

Nostril—single chain stitch with
2 strands of black floss

Mouth—stem stitch with 2 strands
of black floss

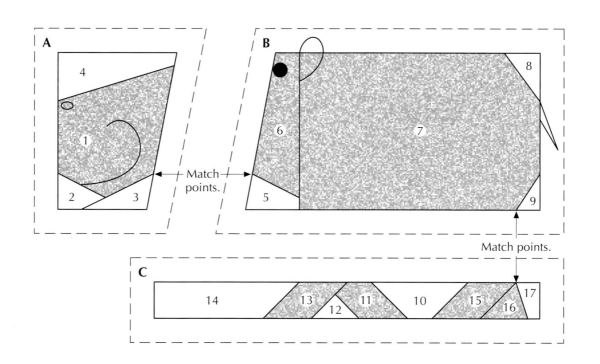

Horned Owl

COLORS

Top of head and wings (Pieces 3, 8, and 14)—brown

Eye patches (Pieces 2 and 4)—gold

Cheeks (Pieces 11 and 17)—cream

Breast (Pieces 6 and 13)—beige

Tail (Pieces 7 and 12)— medium brown

Branch—dark brown

Background fabric

JOINING SECTIONS

1. A + B

2. (A-B) + C. Press the seam allowances toward the top of the block.

3. (A-C) + D. Press the seam allowances toward the top of the block.

SIZE OPTIONS

Finished size: 2½" x 4"

For a 4" x 4" finished size, add 1½"-wide strips to the sides, then trim the block to 4½" x 4½".

For a 5" x 5" finished size, add 2"-wide strips to the sides and 1¼"-wide strips to the top and bottom, then trim the block to 5½" x 5½".

ADDING DETAILS

Eye center—chain stitch with 2 strands of black floss

Circle around eye—chain stitch with 2 strands of yellow floss

Beak—straight stitch with 2 strands of brown floss

Branch—make a folded strip, ¼"-wide finished size, from brown fabric; appliqué in place (see page 11)

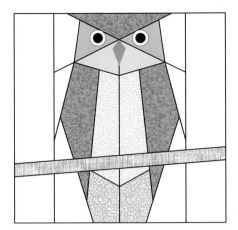

SEE COLOR PHOTO ON PAGE 18

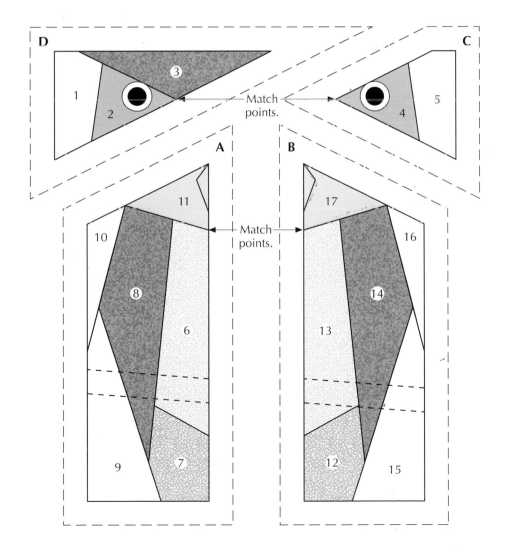

Hummingbird

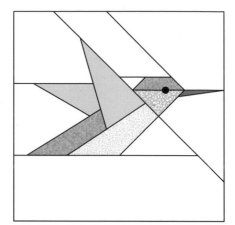

SEE COLOR PHOTOS
ON PAGES 32–33

COLOR

Head and back (Pieces 1 and 10)
—dark green

Wings (Pieces 9 and 12)
—medium green

Throat (Piece 7)—dark pink

Beak (Piece 6)—gray

Breast (Piece 13)—light green

Background fabric

JOINING SECTIONS

1. A + B
2. (A-B) + C

SIZE OPTIONS

Finished size: 4" x 4"

For a 5" x 5" finished size, add
1¼"-wide strips, then trim the block
to 5½" x 5½".

ADDING DETAILS

Eye—chain stitch with 2 strands
of black floss

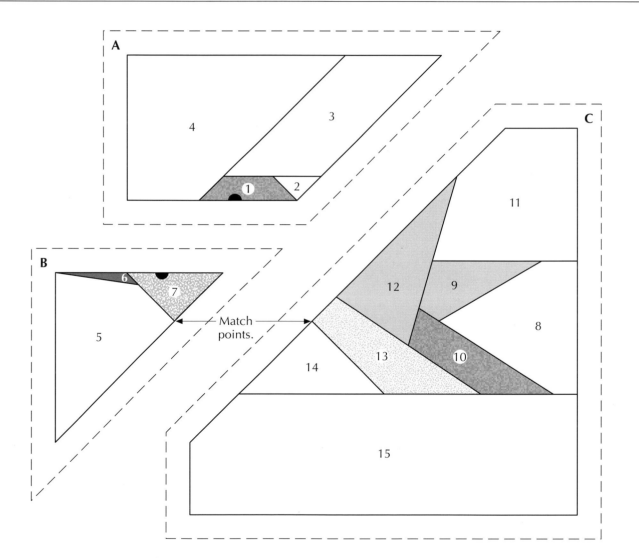

Kangaroo

COLORS

Body—rust or gray
Background fabric

JOINING SECTIONS

1. A + B
2. (A-B) + C + D + E

SIZE OPTIONS

Finished size: 4" x 4"

For a 5" x 5" finished size, add
1¼"-wide strips, then trim the block
to 5½" x 5½".

ADDING DETAILS

Eye—double chain stitch with
2 strands of black floss

Nose—straight stitch with 2 strands
of black floss

Leg curve—stem stitch with
2 strands of floss in a matching color
(or quilt this line)

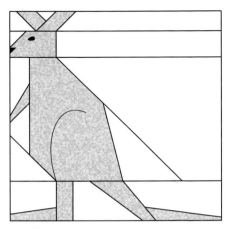

SEE COLOR PHOTO ON PAGE 47

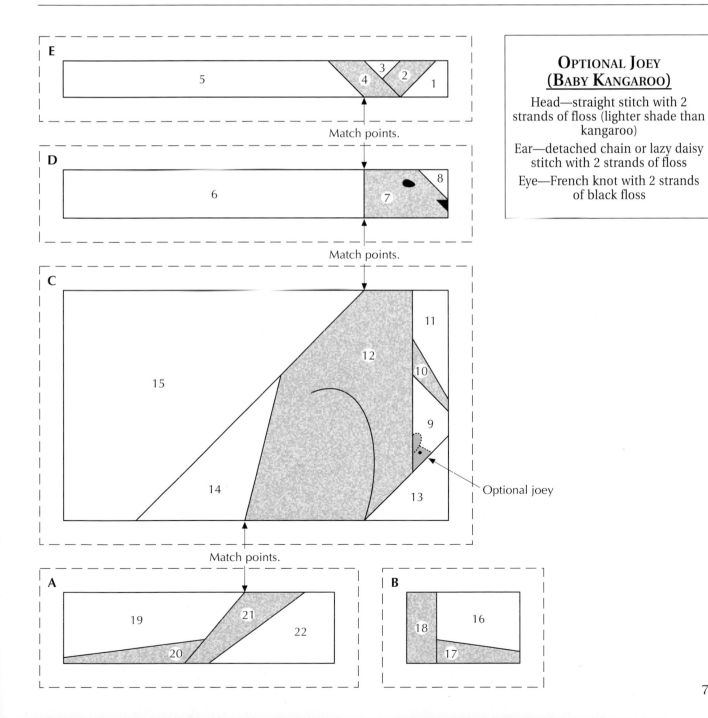

OPTIONAL JOEY (BABY KANGAROO)

Head—straight stitch with 2
strands of floss (lighter shade than
kangaroo)

Ear—detached chain or lazy daisy
stitch with 2 strands of floss

Eye—French knot with 2 strands
of black floss

75

Koala

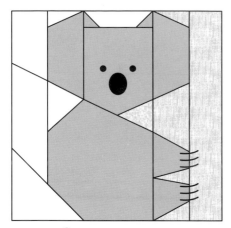

SEE COLOR PHOTOS
ON PAGES 25 AND 47

COLORS

Body—gray
Neck (Piece 5)—light gray or white
Tree—brown
Background fabric

JOINING SECTIONS

1. A + B
2. (A-B) + C

SIZE OPTIONS

Finished size: 4" x 4"

For a 5" x 5" finished size, add
1¼"-wide strips, then trim the block
to 5½" x 5½".

ADDING DETAILS

Nose and eyes—chain stitch with
2 strands of black floss

Claws—stem stitch with 2 strands
of black floss

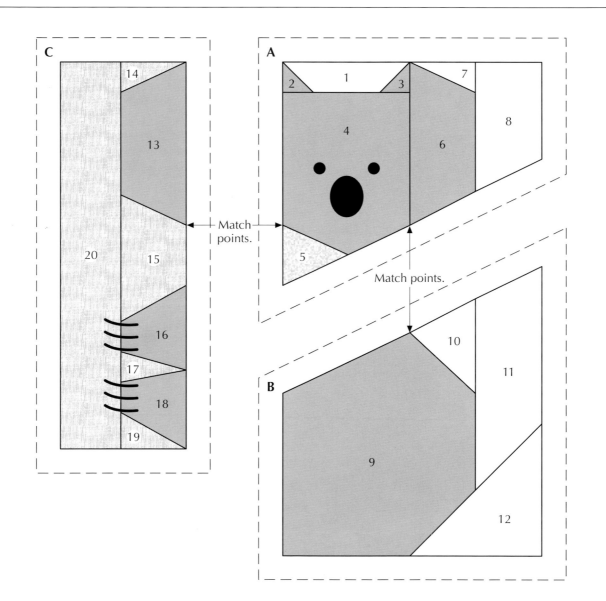

Kookaburra

COLOR

Upper beak—gray
Lower beak—yellow
Head and breast—beige
Wing—brown
Tail—rust
Eye patch and feet—light brown
Background fabric

JOINING SECTIONS

1. A + B
2. (A-B) + C +D

SIZE OPTIONS

Finished size: 4" x 4"

For a 5" x 5" finished size, add
1¼"-wide strips, then trim the block
to 5½" x 5½".

ADDING DETAILS

Eye patch and feet—appliqué using
light brown fabric (see page 11)

Eye—chain stitch with 2 strands
of black floss; buttonhole stitch
edges with 1 strand of brown floss

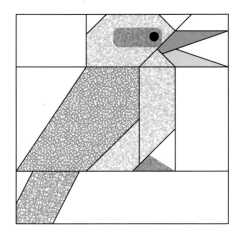

SEE COLOR PHOTO ON PAGE 47

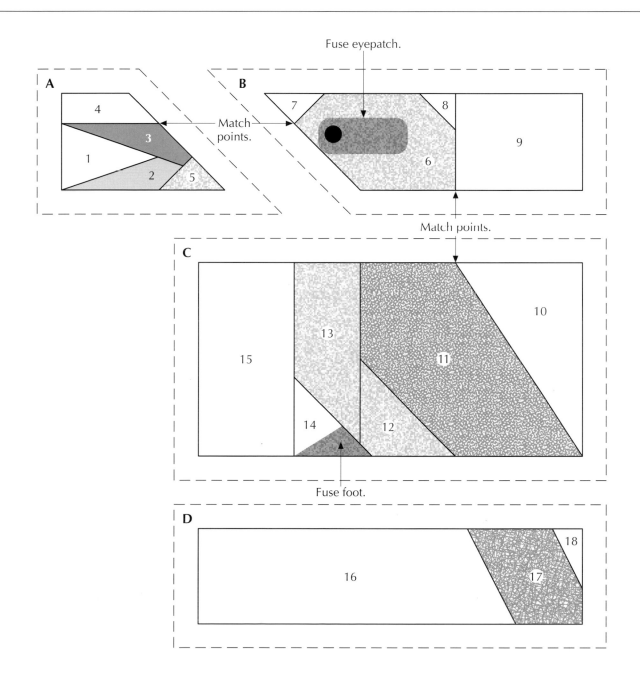

Leopard

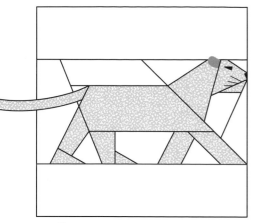

SEE COLOR PHOTO ON PAGE 17

COLOR

Body—light brown with spotty black print

Background fabric

JOINING SECTIONS

A + B + C

SIZE OPTIONS

Finished size: 4" x 2"

For a 4" x 4" finished size, add 1¾"-wide strips to the top and bottom, then trim the block to 4½" x 4½".

For a 5" x 5" finished size, add 1¼"-wide strips to the sides and 2¼"-wide strips to the top and bottom, then trim the block to 5½" x 5½".

NOTE: The tail will extend beyond the side strip.

ADDING DETAILS

Ear—double chain stitch with 4 strands of floss in a matching color

Tail—make a folded strip, ¼" x 2½" finished size (see page 11); appliqué in place

Eye—straight stitch with 2 strands of black floss

Whiskers—straight stitch with 1 strand of black floss

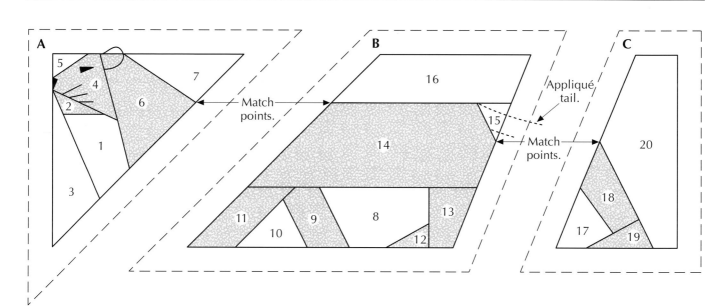

Lion

COLORS

Face and body—light gold
Mane—dark gold
Back foot—medium gold
Background fabric

JOINING SECTIONS

1. A + B
2. (A-B) + C + D

SIZE OPTIONS

Finished size: 4" x 4"

For a 5" x 5" finished size, add
1¼"-wide strips, then trim the block
to 5½" x 5½".

ADDING DETAILS

Ears—chain stitch with 2 strands
of gold floss

Tail—plait with 12 strands
of gold floss (see page 12)

Eyes and nose—straight stitch with
2 strands of black floss

Mouth—stem stitch with 2 strands
of black floss

Chin (optional)—straight stitch with
2 strands of beige floss or appliqué
using beige fabric (see page 11)

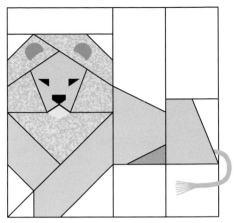

SEE COLOR PHOTOS
ON PAGES 17 AND 48

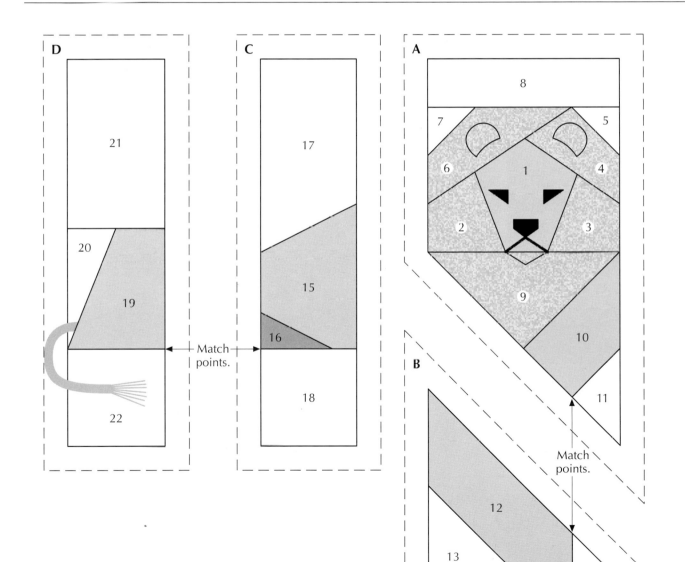

Loon

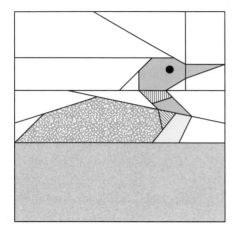

SEE COLOR PHOTO ON PAGE 28

COLORS

Head, beak, and neck
(Pieces 1, 8, and 11)—black

Neckband (Piece 10)
—black-and-white stripe

Lower breast (Piece 16)—white

Breast above wing (Piece 15)
—black-and-white stripe

Back (Piece 14)
—black-and-white print

Water (Piece 20)—green

Background fabric

JOINING SECTIONS

1. A +B
2. C + D
3. (A-B) + (C-D)

SIZE OPTIONS

Finished size: 4" x 4"

For a 5" x 5" finished size, add
1¼"-wide strips, then trim the block
to 5½" x 5½".

ADDING DETAILS

Eye center—double chain stitch with
2 strands of black floss

Outer eye—single chain stitch
around eye center with 2 strands
of red floss

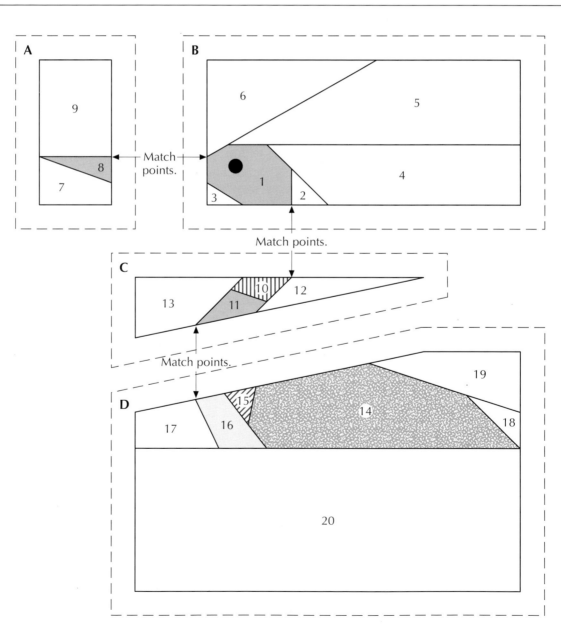

Monkey

Colors

Body and face—light brown
Outer face—dark brown
Background fabric

Joining Sections

1. A + B
2. (A-B) + C + D
3. (A-D) + E

Size Options

Finished size: 4" x 4"

For a 5" x 5" finished size, add
1¼"-wide strips, then trim the block
to 5½" x 5½".

Adding Details

Ears and tail—chain stitch with
2 strands of light brown floss
Feet—chain stitch with 2 strands
of brown floss
Eyes—double chain stitch with
2 strands of black floss
Nostrils—French knot with 1 strand
of black floss
Mouth—stem stitch with 1 strand
of black floss

SEE COLOR PHOTO ON PAGE 17

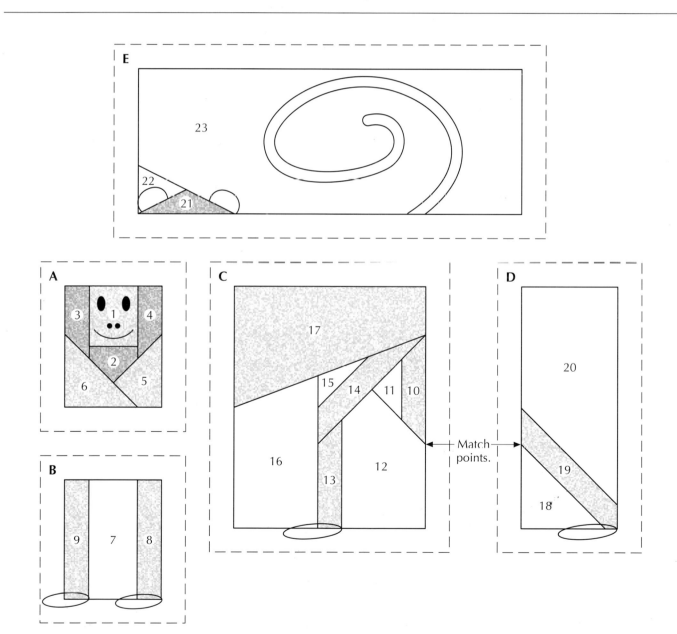

Panda

SEE COLOR PHOTOS
ON PAGES 24–25

COLOR

Ears, upper body, and legs—black
Face and tummy—white
Background fabric

JOINING SECTIONS

1. A + B
2. (A-B) + C
3. (A-C) + D + E

SIZE OPTIONS

Finished size: 4" x 4"

For a 5" x 5" finished size, add
1¼"-wide strips, then trim the block
to 5½" x 5½".

ADDING DETAILS

Eye patches—appliqué using
black fabric (see page 11)

Eyes—single chain stitch with
2 strands of white floss, or use
small white beads

Nose and mouth—straight stitch
with 2 strands of black floss

Bamboo (optional)

Stem—straight stitch with 2 strands
of beige floss

Leaves—Chain stitch with 2 strands
of green floss

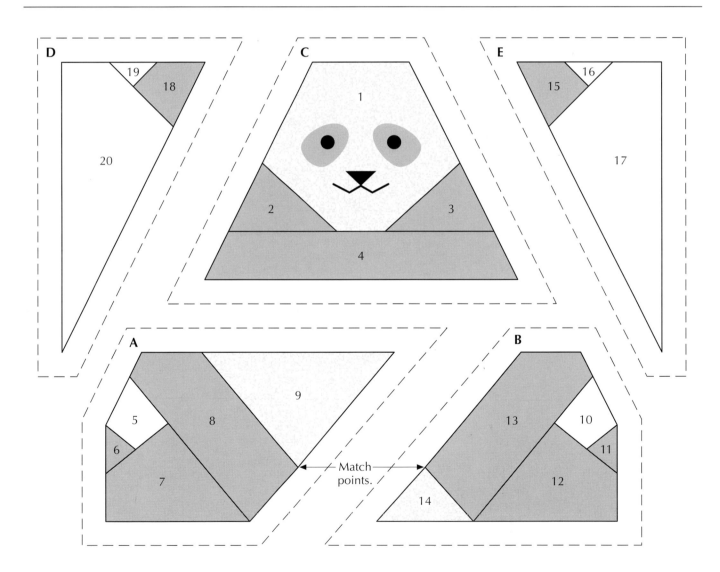

Parrot (Crimson Rosella)

COLORS

Head, breast, and upper tail (Pieces 4, 5, 7, and 14)—red

Cheek, lower wing, and tail (Pieces 1, 6, and 13)—bright blue

Middle wing (Piece 2)—dark blue

Upper wing (Piece 3)—dark red

Beak and feet (Pieces 11 and 12) —light gray or beige

Background fabric

JOINING SECTIONS

1. A + B
2. (A-B) + C

SIZE OPTIONS

Finished size: 4" x 4"

For a 5" x 5" finished size, add 1¼"-wide strips, then trim the block to 5½" x 5½".

ADDING DETAILS

Eye—chain stitch with 2 strands of black floss

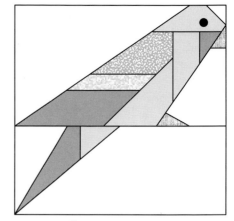

SEE COLOR PHOTO
ON PAGE 36

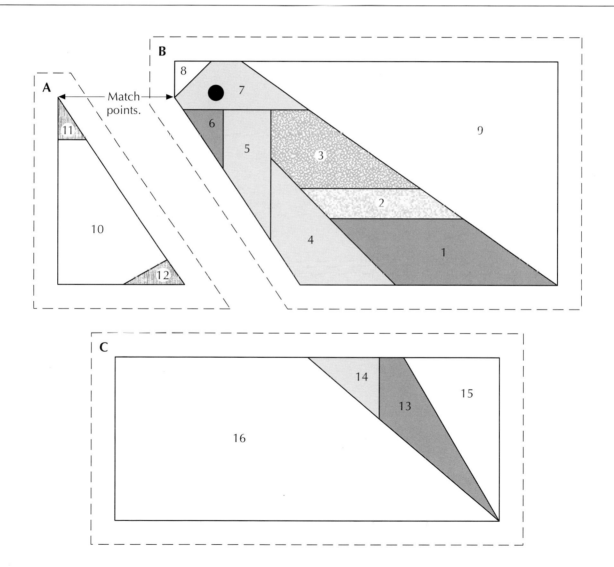

Peacock

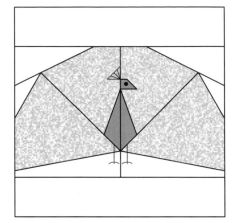

SEE COLOR PHOTO
ON PAGE 27

COLORS

Tail—green or turquoise (Follow arrows if using a directional print.)

Body—blue

Background fabric

JOINING SECTIONS

A + B

SIZE OPTIONS

Finished size: 4" x 2½"

For a 4" x 4" finished size, add 1½"-wide strips to the top and bottom, then trim the block to 4½" x 4½".

For a 5" x 5" finished size, add 1¼"-wide strips to the sides and 2"-wide strips to the top and bottom, then trim the block to 5½" x 5½".

ADDING DETAILS

Head and crest—straight stitch with 2 strands of blue floss

Eye and crest embellishment (if desired)—French knots with 2 strands of contrasting color of floss

Legs—chain stitch with 2 strands of gray floss

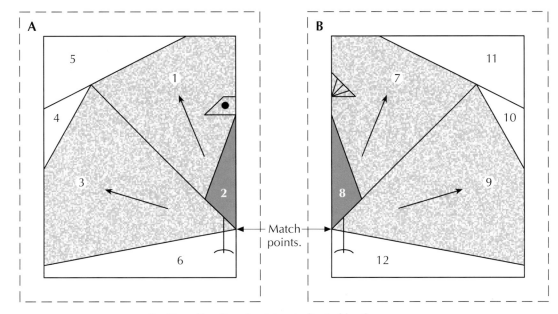

Position directional print as indicated by the arrows.

Pelican

COLORS

Beak—pink
Head and body—white
Wings—black
Water—blue
Background fabric

JOINING SECTIONS

A + B

SIZE OPTIONS

Finished size: 4" x 3"

For a 4" x 4" finished size, add
a 1¾"-wide blue strip to the bottom,
then trim the block to 4½" x 4½".

For a 5" x 5" finished size,
add 1¼"-wide strips to the sides
and top and a 2¼"-wide blue strip
to the bottom, then trim the block
to 5½" x 5½".

ADDING DETAILS

Eye center—chain stitch with
2 strands of black floss
Outer eye—chain stitch with
2 strands of yellow floss

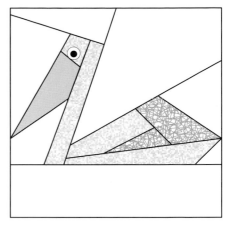

SEE COLOR PHOTO ON PAGE 31

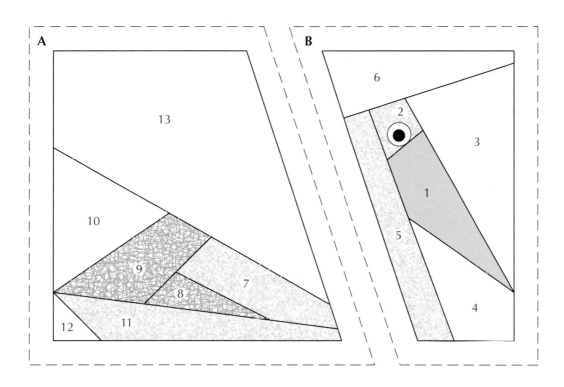

Penguin

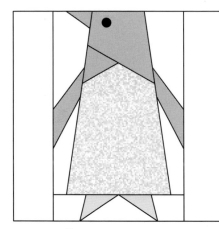

SEE COLOR PHOTOS
ON PAGES 40–41

COLORS

Head and wings—black
Breast—white
Feet—orange or red
Background fabric

JOINING SECTIONS

1. A + B + C
2. (A-C) + D

SIZE OPTIONS

Finished size: 2½" x 4"

For a 4" x 4" finished size, add
1½"-wide strips to the sides, then
trim the block to 4½" x 4½".

For a 5" x 5" finished size, add
2"-wide strips to the sides and
1¼"-wide strips to the top and
bottom, then trim the block
to 5½" x 5½".

ADDING DETAILS

Eye—chain stitch with 2 strands
of white floss

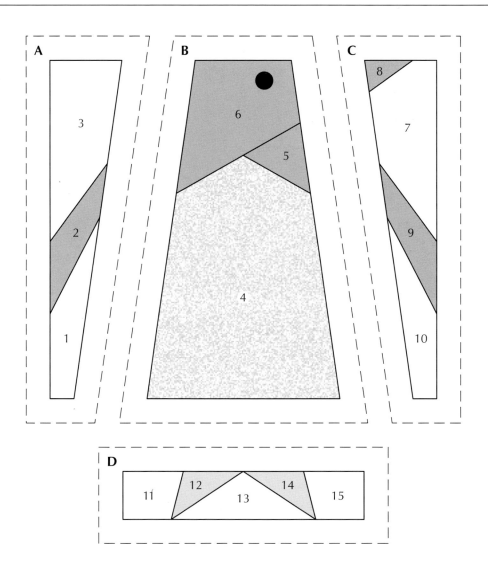

COLORS

Body—light pink
Ears—dark pink
Background fabric

JOINING SECTIONS

A + B

SIZE OPTIONS

Finished size: 4" x 3"

For a 4" x 4" finished size, add 1¼"-wide strips to the top and bottom, then trim the block to 4½" x 4½".

For a 5" x 5" finished size, add 1¼"-wide strips to the sides and 1¾"-wide strips to the top and bottom, then trim the block to 5½" x 5½".

ADDING DETAILS

Ear—appliqué using dark pink fabric (see page 11); buttonhole stitch around edges with 1 strand of dark pink floss

Tail and nose—chain stitch with 2 strands of dark pink floss

Eye—double chain stitch with 2 strands of black floss

Nostrils—single chain stitch with 2 strands of black floss

Mouth—stem stitch with 2 strands of black floss

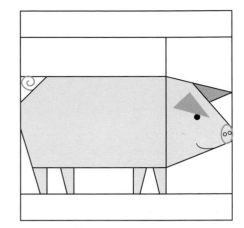

SEE COLOR PHOTOS
ON PAGES 20 AND 44

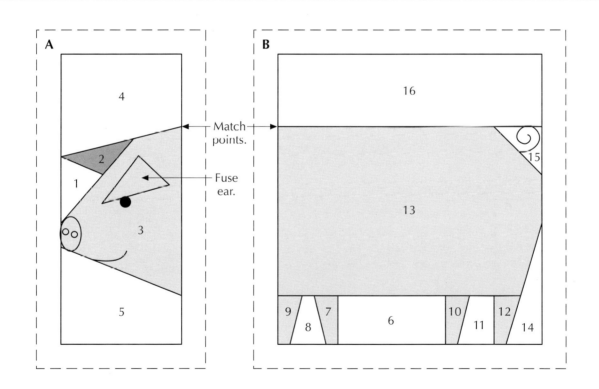

Platypus

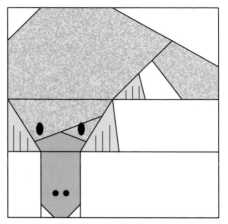

SEE COLOR PHOTO ON PAGE 47

COLORS

Body—light brown
Feet—medium brown
Bill—dark brown
Background fabric

JOINING SECTIONS

A + B + C

SIZE OPTIONS

Finished size: 4" x 4"

For a 5" x 5" finished size, add
1¼"-wide strips, then trim the block
to 5½" x 5½".

ADDING DETAILS

Eye—chain stitch with 2 strands
of black floss

Nostrils—single chain stitch with
2 strands of black floss

Lines on feet—stem stitch with
2 strands of black floss

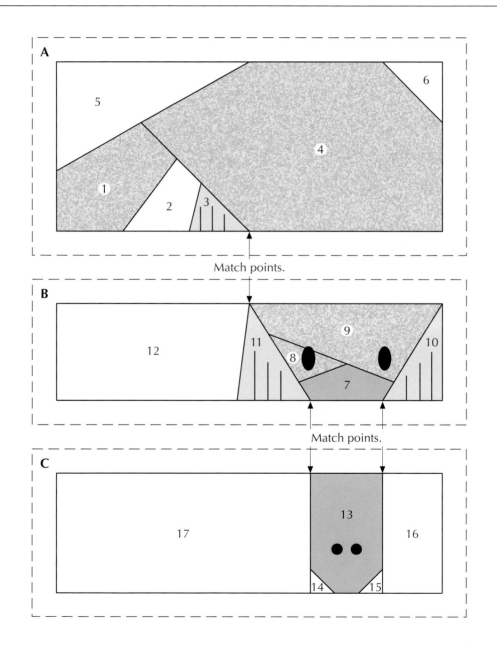

COLORS

Body—white
Background fabric

JOINING SECTIONS

A + B

SIZE OPTIONS

Finished size: 4" x 2½"

For a 4" x 4" finished size, add 1½"-wide strips to the top and bottom, then trim the block to 4½" x 4½".

For a 5" x 5" finished size, add 1¼"-wide strips to the sides and 2"-wide strips to the top and bottom, then trim the block to 5½" x 5½".

ADDING DETAILS

Eye—chain stitch with 2 strands of black floss

Nose—straight stitch with 2 strands of black floss

Ear—outline in stem stitch with 1 strand of black floss

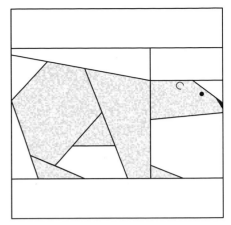

SEE COLOR PHOTO ON PAGE 17

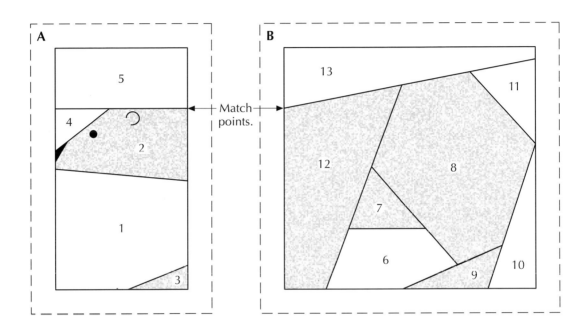

Puffin

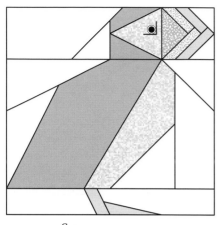

See color photo on page 41

Colors

Body and back of head (Pieces 9, 10, and 13)—black

Face and breast (Pieces 8 and 14)—white

Beak (Piece 1)—blue

Beak (Pieces 2 and 3)—yellow

Beak and feet (Pieces 4, 5, 21, and 22)—red

Background fabric

Joining Sections

A + B + C

Size Options

Finished size: 4" x 4"

For a 5" x 5" finished size, add 1¼"-wide strips, then trim the block to 5½" x 5½".

Adding Details

Eye center—chain stitch with 2 strands of black floss

Outer eye—chain stitch with 1 strand of red floss

Lines in front of and below eye —stem stitch with 1 strand of black floss

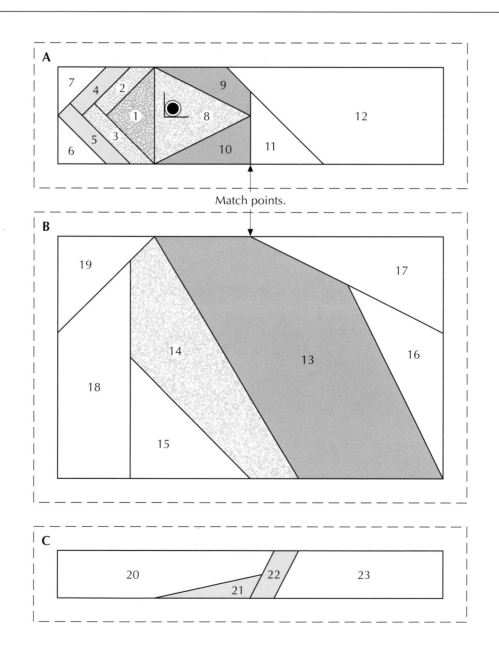

Rabbit

COLORS

Body—white
Background fabric

JOINING SECTIONS

1. A + B
2. (A-B) + C

SIZE OPTIONS

Finished size: 4" x 3"

For a 4" x 4" finished size, add 1¼"-wide strips to the top and bottom, then trim the block to 4½" x 4½".

For a 5" x 5" finished size, add 1¼"-wide strips to the sides and 1¾"-wide strips to the top and bottom, then trim the block to 5½" x 5½".

ADDING DETAILS

Eye—chain stitch with 2 strands of pink floss
Whiskers—straight stitch with 1 strand of gray floss

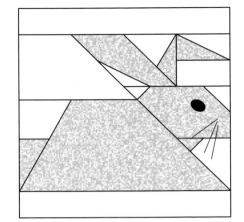

SEE COLOR PHOTO ON PAGE 20

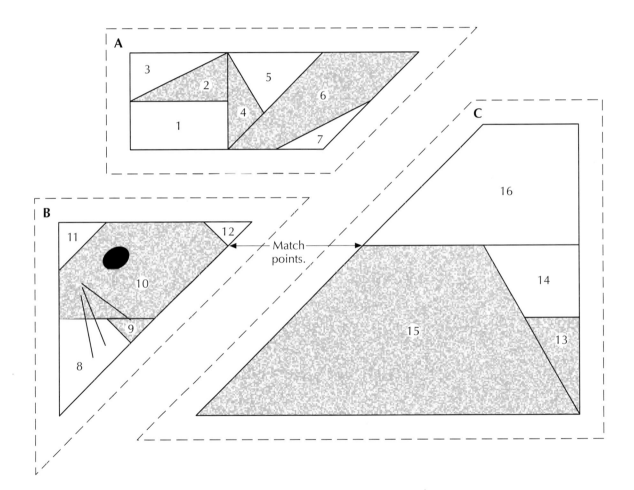

Match points.

Rhinoceros

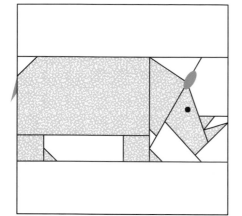

SEE COLOR PHOTOS ON PAGES 17 AND 48

COLORS

Rhinoceros—gray or light brown
Background fabric

JOINING SECTIONS

1. A + B
2. (A-B) + C

SIZE OPTIONS

Finished size: 4" x 2"

For a 4" x 4" finished size, add a 1¾"-wide strip to the top and bottom, then trim the block to 4½" x 4½".

For a 5" x 5" finished size, add 1¼"-wide strips to the sides and 2¼"-wide strips to the top and bottom, then trim the block to 5½" x 5½".

ADDING DETAILS

Ear—long double chain stitch with 4 strands of floss in a matching color

Tail—straight stitch with 4 strands of floss in a matching color

Eye—French knot with 2 strands of black floss

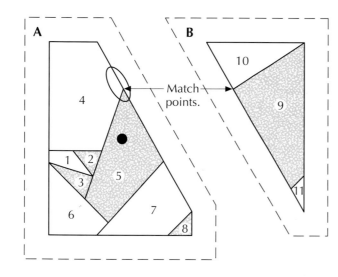

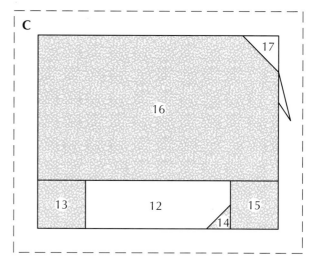

Rooster

COLORS

Tail and neck—bright print
Body—black or rust
Beak—yellow
Comb and wattle—red
Background fabric

JOINING SECTIONS

A + B + C

SIZE OPTIONS

Finished size: 4" x 4"
For a 5" x 5" finished size, add
1¼"-wide strips, then trim the block
to 5½" x 5½".

ADDING DETAILS

Comb and wattle—appliqué using
red fabric (see page 11); buttonhole
stitch with 1 strand of red floss

Eye—chain stitch with 2 strands
of black floss

Legs—chain stitch with 2 strands
of yellow floss

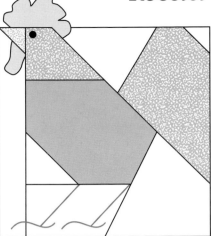

SEE COLOR PHOTOS
ON PAGES 38–39 AND 44

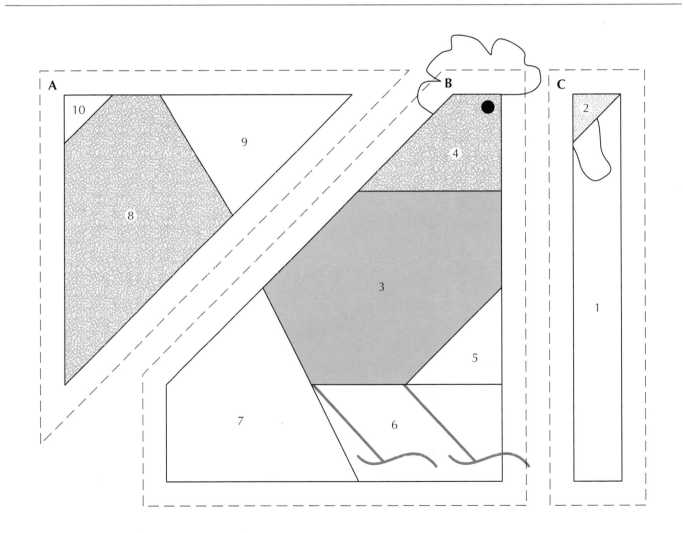

Scotty Dog

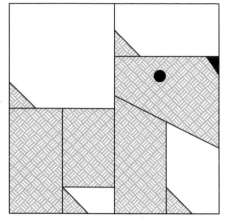

SEE COLOR PHOTO ON PAGE 35

COLORS

Dog—plaid, check, or black
(Directional fabrics work well in this
design because all seams are sewn
at 90° or 45° angles.)

Background fabric

JOINING SECTIONS

1. A + B
2. C + D
3. (A-B) + (C-D)

SIZE OPTIONS

Finished size: 4" x 4"

For a 5" x 5" finished size, add
1¼"-wide strips, then trim the block
to 5½" x 5½".

ADDING DETAILS

Eye—chain stitch with 2 strands
of black floss or use a small button

Nose (optional)—straight stitch
with 2 strands of black floss; the
nose may not show against
a black background

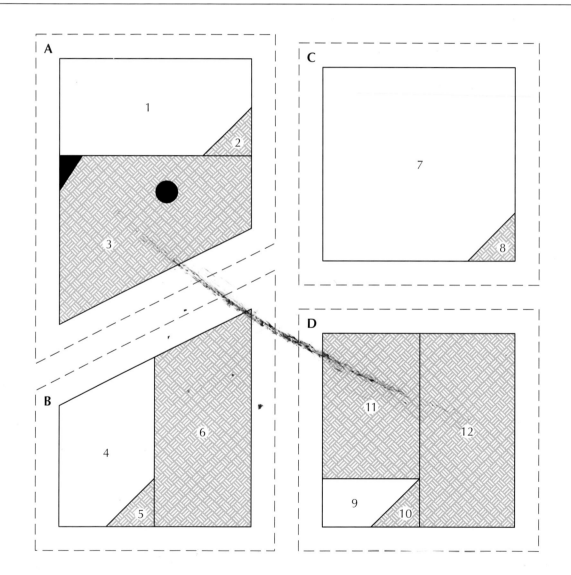

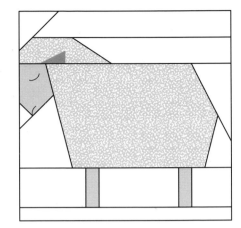

COLORS

Body—beige
Face and legs—light brown
Grass (Piece 16)—green
Background fabric

JOINING SECTIONS

A + B + C

SIZE OPTIONS

Finished size: 4" x 4"

For a 5" x 5" finished size, add
1¼"-wide strips, then trim the block
to 5½" x 5½".

ADDING DETAILS

Ear—chain stitch with 2 strands
of light brown floss

Eye and mouth—stem stitch with
2 strands of black floss

SEE COLOR PHOTO ON PAGE 44

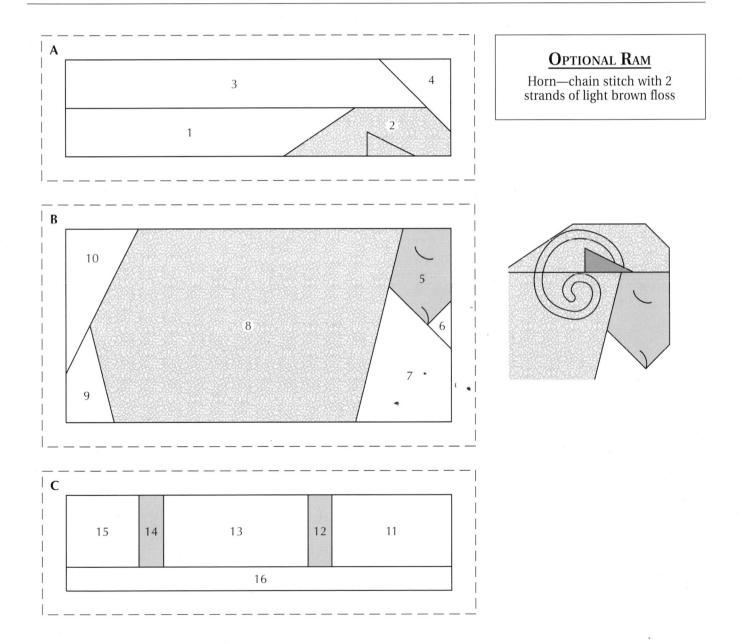

OPTIONAL RAM

Horn—chain stitch with 2
strands of light brown floss

Tiger

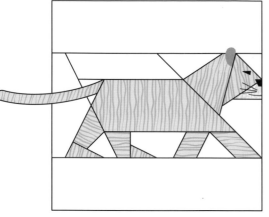

SEE COLOR PHOTO ON PAGE 17

COLORS

Body and head—orange-and-black stripe (Stripe direction should match illustration.)

Chin—white

Background fabric

JOINING SECTIONS

A + B + C

SIZE OPTIONS

Finished size: 4" x 2"

For a 4" x 4" finished size, add 1¾"-wide strips to the top and bottom, then trim the block to 4½" x 4½".

For a 5" x 5" finished size, add 1¼"-wide strips to the sides and 2¼"-wide strips to the top and bottom, then trim the block to 5½" x 5½".

NOTE: The tail will extend beyond the side strip.

ADDING DETAILS

Tail—make a folded strip, ¼" x 2½" finished, with stripes going around the tail (see page 11); appliqué in place

Inner ear—double chain stitch with 4 strands of white floss

Ear outline and mouth—stem stitch with 1 strand of black floss

Eye and nose—straight stitch with 2 strands of black floss

Whiskers—straight stitch with 1 strand of black floss

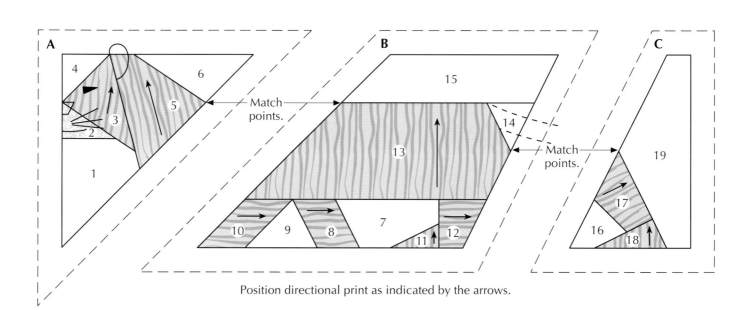

Position directional print as indicated by the arrows.

Tortoise

COLORS

Shell—brown print
Head and legs—brown
Background fabric

JOINING SECTIONS

1. A + B
2. (A-B) + C

SIZE OPTIONS

Finished size: 4" x 2"

For a 4" x 4" finished size, add
1¾"-wide strips to the top and
bottom, then trim the block
to 4½" x 4½".

For a 5" x 5" finished size, add
1¼"-wide strips to the sides and
2¼"-wide strips to the top and
bottom, then trim the block
to 5½" x 5½".

ADDING DETAILS

Eye—double chain stitch with
2 strands of black floss
Mouth—stem stitch with 1 strand
of black floss

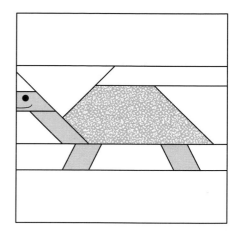

SEE COLOR PHOTO ON PAGE 17
*NOTE: This block is reversed
in the Ark Quilt.*

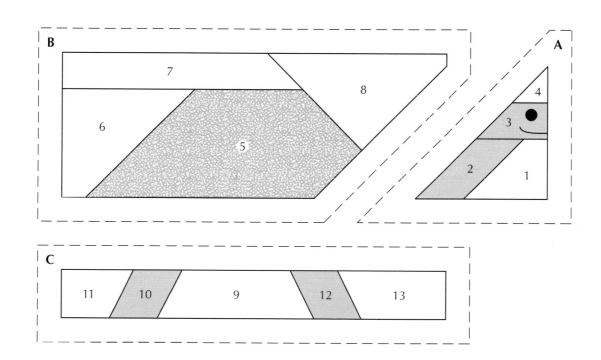

Toucan

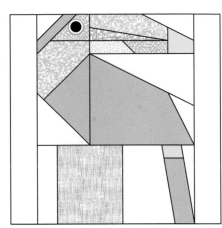

SEE COLOR PHOTO ON PAGE 23

COLORS

Beak (Piece 1)—green

Beak and eye patch
(Pieces 2 and 13)—bright blue

Beak (Piece 3)—orange

Beak and neck (Pieces 4 and 11)—yellow

Beak and upper tail
(Pieces 5 and 17) —red

Top of head, body, and lower tail
(Pieces 7, 10, 14, and 16)—black

Post (Piece 20)—gray or brown

Background fabric

JOINING SECTION

1. A + B
2. (A-B) + C
3. (A-C) + D

SIZE OPTIONS

Finished size: 3" x 4"

For a 4" x 4" finished size, add
1¼"-wide strips to the sides, then
trim the block to 4½" x 4½".

For a 5" x 5" finished size, add
1¾"-wide strips to the sides and
1¼"-wide strips to the top and
bottom, then trim the block
to 5½" x 5½".

ADDING DETAILS

Eye center—chain stitch with
2 strands of black floss

Outer eye—chain stitch with
2 strands of white floss

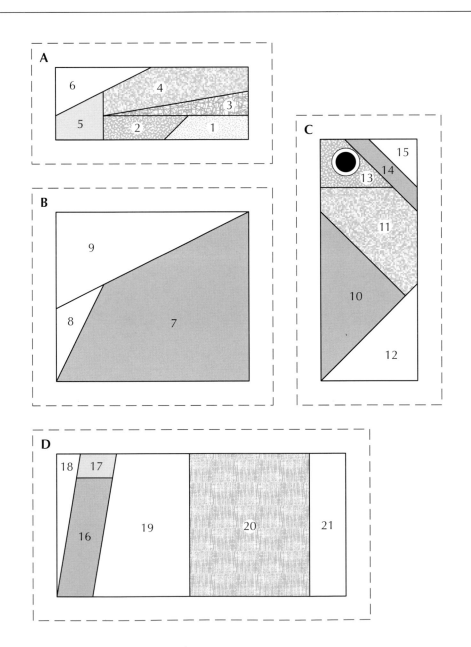

Turkey

COLORS

Neck (Piece 2)—red

Head (Piece 3)—gray

Back and breast
(Pieces 8 and 14)—black

Upper wing (Piece 13)—brown

Lower wing
(Piece 12)—black-and-white print

Tail (Piece 16)—rust

Background fabric

JOINING SECTIONS

1. A + B
2. (A-B) + C
3. (A-C) + D

SIZE OPTIONS

Finished size: 4" x 4"

For a 5" x 5" finished size, add
1¼"-wide strips, then trim the block
to 5½" x 5½".

ADDING DETAILS

Eye—chain stitch with 2 strands
of black floss

Beard on front of breast—straight
stitch with 1 strand of black floss

Legs—chain stitch with 3 strands
of gray floss

Snood (flesh over beak)—chain stitch
with 2 strands of red floss

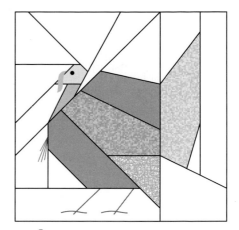

SEE COLOR PHOTO ON PAGE 34

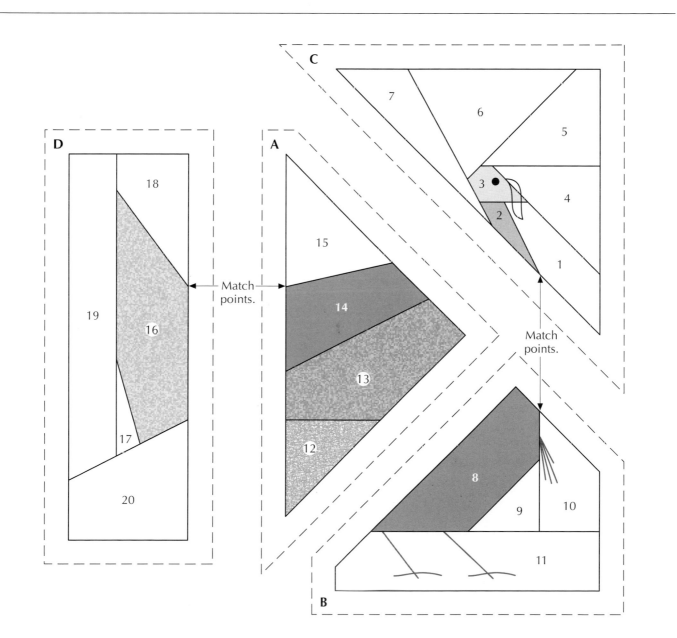

Match points.

Match points.

Wombat

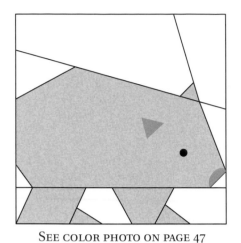

COLORS

Wombat—brown
Background fabric

JOINING SECTIONS

A + B + C

SIZE OPTIONS

Finished size: 4" x 4"

For a 5" x 5" finished size, add
1¼"-wide strips, then trim the block
to 5½" x 5½".

ADDING DETAILS

Eye and nose—chain stitch with
2 strands of black floss

Ear—chain stitch with 2 strands
of dark brown floss

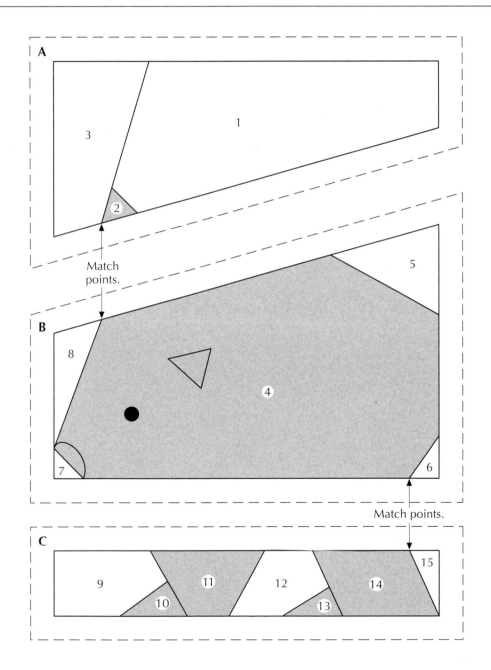

Zebra

Colors

Body—black-and-white stripe
(Stripe direction should
match illustration.)

Background fabric

Joining Sections

1. A + B
2. (A-B) + C
3. (A-C) + D

Size Options

Finished size: 4" x 3"

For a 4" x 4" finished size, add
1¼"-wide strips to the top and
bottom, then trim the block
to 4½" x 4½".

For a 5" x 5" finished size, add
1¼"-wide strips to the sides and
1¾"-wide strips to the top and
bottom, then trim the block
to 5½" x 5½".

Adding Details

Ear—double chain stitch with
4 strands of white floss; to outline,
stem stitch with 1 strand
of black floss

Tail—plait with 12 strands of black
floss (see page 12)

Eye—double chain stitch with
2 strands of black floss

Mane—buttonhole stitch with
2 strands of black floss

Nose—straight stitch with 2 strands
of black floss

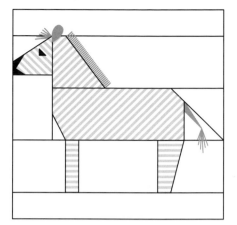

SEE COLOR PHOTO ON PAGE 17

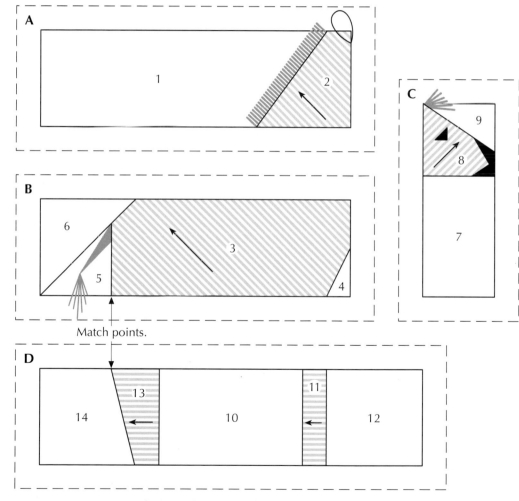

Match points.

Position directional print as indicated by the arrows.

Ark Quilt

FINISHED SIZE: 41" X 51"

SEE COLOR PHOTO ON PAGE 17

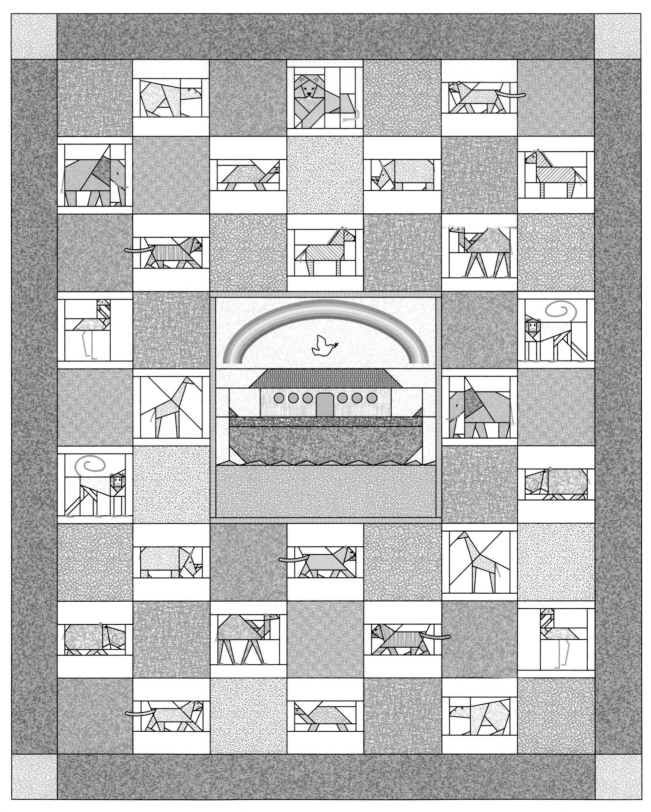

MATERIALS: 44"-WIDE FABRIC

1 yd. lightweight interfacing for foundation (nonfusible, nonwoven)

Assorted fabrics and embroidery floss for 13 animal blocks (Refer to "Blocks," pages 49–101.)

13 assorted light prints, each 9" x 21", for animal backgrounds

14 assorted medium and dark prints, each 6" x 12", for alternate blocks

¼ yd. light blue print for sky

⅛ yd. each or small pieces of red, light brown, dark brown, green, beige, and blue prints for roof, walls, deck, windows, and door

¼ yd. brown print for ark hull (or 4" x 15" scrap)

¼ yd. medium blue print for water

¼ yd. dark green print for ark block border (or 2" x 32" strip)

1 fat quarter (18" x 22" piece) each of red, orange, yellow, green, blue, and violet solids for rainbow (or one ¾" x 20" bias-cut strip of each color)

Dark brown, white, black, light brown, and green embroidery floss

Scrap of white solid for dove

Small piece of paper-backed fusible web for appliqué

½ yd. dark blue print for border

¼ yd. light red print for corner squares (or 4" x 15" strip)

45" x 55" piece of thin batting

1½ yds. backing fabric

½ yd. red print for binding

BLOCK ASSEMBLY

Animal and Alternate Blocks: 5" x 5"
Refer to "Blocks," pages 49–101

1. Choose 13 animal blocks and make 2 of each, reversing 1 of each pair. *Use the same background print for each pair.* (To make the lioness, follow the instructions for the Tiger block (page 96) using gold fabric.) Add strips of background fabric to the blocks as required, then trim each block to 5½" x 5½". Finish each animal with appliqué and embroidery as described in the block instructions.

2. From each of the 14 assorted medium and dark prints, cut two 5½" x 5½" squares for alternate blocks.

Ark Block
15" x 15"

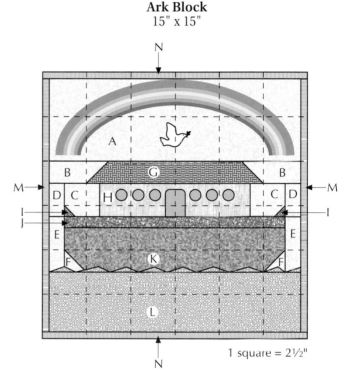

1 square = 2½"

1. From the light blue print (for sky), cut:
   A—1 rectangle, 5⅛" x 14¾"
   B—2 rectangles, each 1¾" x 4¼"

   Place the B rectangles right sides together. Trim one end at a 45° angle.

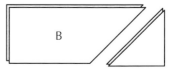

   C—2 squares, each 2⅜" x 2⅜"
   D—2 rectangles, each 1⅜" x 2⅜"
   E—2 rectangles, each 1⅜" x 3⅝"
   F—2 squares, each 1¾" x 1¾"

2. From the red print (for roof), cut:
    G—1 rectangle, 1¾" x 11¼"
    Trim both ends at a 45° angle.

3. From the light brown print (for walls), cut:
    H—1 rectangle, 2⅜" x 9¼"
4. From the dark brown print (for upper deck), cut:
    I—2 squares, each 1⅛" x 1⅛"
    J—1 rectangle, 1⅛" x 13"
    Draw a diagonal line on the wrong side of each I square. Place an I square on each C square as shown, right sides together, and stitch on the line. Trim the seam allowances, flip, and press.

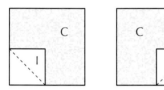

5. From the brown print (for hull), cut:
    K—1 rectangle, 3" x 13"
    Draw a diagonal line on the wrong side of each F square. Place the F squares on the K rectangle as shown, right sides together, and stitch on the line. Trim the seam allowances, flip, and press.

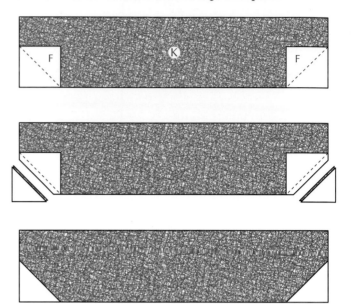

6. From the medium blue print (for water), cut:
    L—1 rectangle, 4¾" x 15⅛" (includes 1" extra for waves)
7. From the dark green print (for borders), cut:
    M—2 strips, each ⅞" x 14¾"
    N—2 strips, each ⅞" x 15½"
8. Arrange the Ark block. Sew the pieces into horizontal rows, then join the rows.
9. On one long edge of rectangle L, cut gentle waves (about ½" deep) for water. Turn under a ⅛"-wide seam allowance and appliqué piece L below the ark hull. Trim the finished block to 14¾" x 14¾".
10. Sew the M strips to the sides of the block, then sew the N strips to the top and bottom. The block should measure 15½" x 15½".
11. Cut 1 bias strip each from the red, orange, yellow, green, blue, and violet solids, each ¾" x 20". Referring to the photo on page 17, join the rainbow strips in the order shown, beginning with the red strip. To make a curve, stretch the strips a little as you sew, and always sew in the same direction. Trim the seam allowances to ⅛", then press with steam to curve. Trim the ends, turn the edges under ⅛", then appliqué to A.

12. Using the window templates below, cut six 1⅜" circles from the beige print and one ⅞" circle from heavy paper. Baste around the edge of each fabric circle, leaving long tails. Center the paper circle on the wrong side of a fabric circle, then pull the thread tails to gather the fabric around the paper. Press. Remove the basting thread and paper circle, then trim the seam allowance to ⅛". Referring to the quilt photo, baste the window on the ark and then appliqué in place. Repeat for the remaining windows. Using 2 strands of dark brown floss, outline the windows with a chain stitch (page 13).

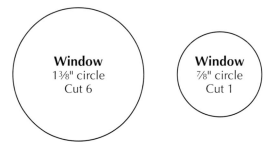

Window
1⅜" circle
Cut 6

Window
⅞" circle
Cut 1

13. To make the door, cut a 1½" x 2" rectangle from a blue scrap. Round the corners on one short side. Turn under a ⅛"-wide seam allowance, then appliqué the door to the ark.

14. Trace the dove on the paper side of paper-backed fusible web, then iron the web onto a scrap of white fabric. Cut out the dove, then fuse it above the ark. Using 1 strand of white floss, outline the dove with a buttonhole stitch (page 12). Using 2 strands of black floss, make a French knot (page 13) for the eye. Using 2 strands of light brown floss, embroider the branch with a stem stitch (page 13). Using 2 strands of green floss, embroider the leaves with a double chain stitch (page 13).

Dove
Trace onto fusible web.

Quilt Top Assembly

1. Arrange the ark, animal, and alternate blocks, balancing colors and pairs of animals. Refer to the quilt photo for ideas.
2. Sew the blocks together in rows, then join the rows.
3. From the dark blue print, cut 4 strips, each 3½" x 44". Measure your quilt top through the center to determine its width and length.

   Cut 2 strips, each 35½" long (or the width of your quilt top if different), for the top and bottom borders.

   Join the remaining pieces, trimming to make 2 strips, each 45½" long (or the length of your quilt top if different), for the side borders.
4. From the light red print, cut 1 strip, 3½" wide; cross-cut the strip to make 4 squares, each 3½" x 3½" (corner squares).
5. Sew a corner square to each end of the top and bottom border strips. Sew the side border strips to the quilt top, then add the top and bottom border strips.

Quilt Finishing

1. Layer the quilt top with batting and backing; baste.
2. Quilt by machine or by hand.
3. From the red print for binding, cut 5 strips, each 2½" wide. Join strips as required to make a binding for the quilt. Press the strips in half lengthwise. Bind the quilt.

Farm Quilt

FINISHED SIZE: 26" x 26"

SEE COLOR PHOTO ON PAGE 44

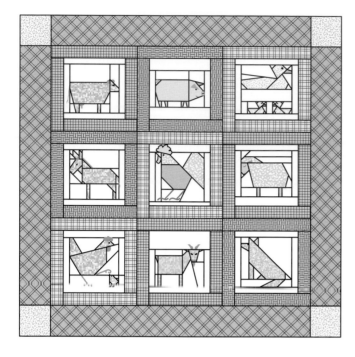

TIP

Use a variety of prints and plaids to give this quilt an informal, Country look.

MATERIALS: 44"-WIDE FABRIC

½ yd. lightweight interfacing for foundation (nonfusible, nonwoven)

¼ yd. each of 9 different prints for backgrounds (or assorted 9" x 9" scraps)

Assorted fabrics and embroidery floss for 9 farm animals (Refer to "Blocks," pages 49–101.)

⅛ yd. each of 9 different plaids for sashing (or 9 strips, each 1½" x 26")

¼ yd. green print for border

¼ yd. mustard print for corner squares (or a 4" x 15" strip)

¼ yd. dark red plaid for binding

30" x 30" piece of thin batting

1 yd. for backing fabric

Small piece of paper-backed fusible web for appliqué

BLOCK ASSEMBLY

1. Referring to the photo on page 44 and to the illustration at left, trace and construct the blocks, using a different background print for each animal. (If you use the hen and duck blocks, you can add a chick and ducklings to the bottom of the blocks if desired.) Add strips of background fabric to the blocks as required, then trim each block to 5½" x 5½". Finish each animal with appliqué and embroidery as described in the block instructions.

2. From the 9 plaids, cut 1½"-wide strips; crosscut *each* strip to make:

    1 strip, 1½" x 5½"
    2 strips, each 1½" x 6½"
    1 strip, 1½" x 7½"

3. Sew strips to each animal block, working log-cabin fashion as shown. For a Country feel, mix up strips of similar colors.

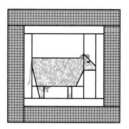

QUILT TOP ASSEMBLY

1. Arrange the blocks as shown in the illustration at left.

2. Sew the blocks together in rows, then join the rows.

3. Measure your quilt top through the center to determine its width and length. From the green print, cut 4 strips, each 3" x 21½" (or match the length of your quilt top if different), for borders. Join 2 border strips to the sides of the quilt top.

4. From the mustard print, cut 1 strip, 3" wide; crosscut the strip to make 4 corner squares, each 3" x 3".

5. Sew the corner squares to the top and bottom border strips, then sew the border strips to the quilt top.

QUILT FINISHING

1. Layer the quilt top with batting and backing; baste.

2. Quilt by machine or by hand.

3. From the dark red plaid, cut 4 strips, each 2" wide. Press the strips in half lengthwise. Bind the quilt.

North American Animals Quilt

FINISHED SIZE: 26" X 26"
ANIMAL BLOCKS: 5 BLOCKS, EACH 5" X 5"
PUSS IN THE CORNER BLOCKS: 4 FULL BLOCKS,
EACH 5" X 5", AND 8 HALF-BLOCKS, EACH 5" X 2½"
SEE COLOR PHOTO ON PAGE 46

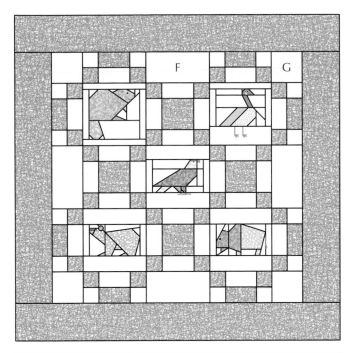

MATERIALS: 44"-WIDE FABRIC

¼ yd. lightweight interfacing for foundation
   (nonfusible, nonwoven)

¾ yd. light blue print for background

Assorted fabrics and embroidery floss for 5
   North American animals (Refer to "Blocks,"
   pages 49–101.)

½ yd. theme print for Puss in the Corner blocks
   and for borders

¼ yd. dark green print for binding

30" x 30" piece of thin batting

1 yd. backing fabric

Small piece of paper-backed fusible web for
   appliqué

BLOCK ASSEMBLY

1. Referring to the photo on page 46 and the illustration above, trace and construct the animal blocks, using the light blue print for the background. Add strips of background fabric to the blocks as required, then trim each block to 5½" x 5½". Finish each animal with appliqué and embroidery as described in the block instructions.

2. From the light blue print, cut:
   3 strips, each 1¾" wide; crosscut the strips to make:
      A—24 rectangles, each 1¾" x 3"
      D—16 squares, each 1¾" x 1¾"
   2 strips, each 3" wide; crosscut the strips to make:
      F—4 rectangles, each 3" x 5½"
      G—4 squares, each 3" x 3"

3. From the theme print, cut:
   2 strips, each 1¾" wide; crosscut the strips to make:
      C—24 squares, each 1¾" x 1¾"
   1 strip, 3" wide; crosscut the strip to make:
      B—4 squares, each 3" x 3"
      E—8 rectangles, each 1¾" x 3" (If the fabric is directional, cut 4 vertical rectangles and 4 horizontal rectangles.)

4. Make 4 full pieced blocks and 4 half blocks as shown. (If the fabric is directional, make sure the fabric placement is consistent for all the blocks.)

Pieced block

Half block

QUILT TOP ASSEMBLY

1. Referring to the illustration at left, arrange the animal blocks, pieced blocks, half blocks, and corner squares as shown.

2. Sew the blocks together in rows, then join the rows.

3. Measure your quilt top through the center to determine its width and length. From the theme print, cut 3 strips, each 3½" x 44". Crosscut the strips to make:
   2 strips, each 3½" x 20½" (or match the length of your quilt top if different), for side borders
   2 strips, each 3½" x 26½" (or match the width of your quilt top if different), for top and bottom borders

4. Sew the side outer border strips to the quilt top, then add the top and bottom border strips.

QUILT FINISHING

1. Layer the quilt top with batting and backing; baste.

2. Quilt by machine or by hand.

3. From the dark green print, cut 4 strips, each 2" wide. Press the strips in half lengthwise. Bind the quilt.

Australian Animals Quilt

FINISHED SIZE: 21½" x 28½"

SEE COLOR PHOTO ON PAGE 47

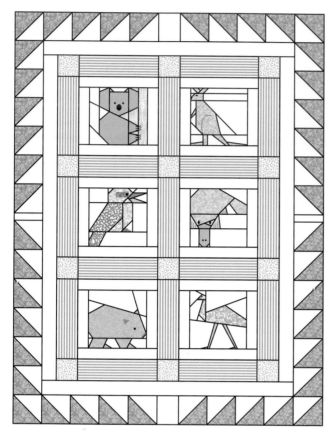

MATERIALS: 44"-WIDE FABRIC

¼ yd. lightweight interfacing for foundation (nonfusible, nonwoven)

¾ yd. light blue print for background of blocks and pieced border

Assorted fabrics and embroidery floss for 6 Australian animals (Refer to "Blocks," pages 49–101.)

½ yd. dark blue print for sashing and binding (If you use a print with a lengthwise stripe, as shown, you will need 1 yd.)

⅛ yd. light brown print for corner squares in sashing (or a 2" x 24" strip)

¼ yd., total, of assorted blue prints for pieced border

26" x 33" piece of thin batting

1 yd. backing fabric

Small piece of paper-backed fusible web for appliqué

BLOCK ASSEMBLY

1. Referring to the photo on page 47 and to the illustration at left, trace and construct the animal blocks, using the light blue print as background.
2. Add 2¼"-wide strips of background fabric to the blocks, then trim each block to 6" x 6". Finish each animal with appliqué and embroidery as described in the block instructions.

QUILT TOP ASSEMBLY

1. From the dark blue print, cut 3 strips, each 2" wide; crosscut the strips to make 17 sashing strips, each 2" x 6".
2. From the light brown print, cut 1 strip, 2" x 24"; crosscut the strip to make 12 squares, each 2" x 2".
3. Arrange the blocks, sashing strips, and corner squares.
4. Sew the blocks, sashing strips, and corner squares together in rows, then join the rows to make the center of the quilt top. Measure the quilt top through the center to determine its length and width.

BORDER ASSEMBLY

1. From the light blue print, cut:
   2 strips, each 1½" wide. Crosscut the strips to make:
   2 strips, each 1½" x 18" (or match the length of the quilt top if different), for inner side borders
   2 strips, each 1½" x 23" (or match the width of the quilt top if different), for inner top and bottom borders
   2 strips, each 2⅞" wide; crosscut the strips to make 22 squares, each 2⅞" x 2⅞". Cut each square in half diagonally to make 44 half-square triangles for the pieced outer border.
   From the scraps, cut one 2½" x 6" strip; crosscut the strip to make:
   2 rectangles, each 2" x 2½", for outer borders
   2 rectangles, each 1" x 2½", for outer borders
2. From each of the assorted blue prints, cut enough 2⅞"-wide strips to make 22 squares, each 2⅞" x 2⅞". Cut each square in half diagonally to make 44 half-square triangles for the pieced outer border.
3. Sew the 1½" x 18" light blue inner border strips to the sides of the quilt top, then sew the 1½" x 23" border strips to the top and bottom.

4. Join the light blue and the assorted blue half-square triangles to make 22 squares.

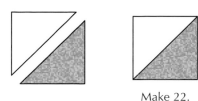

Make 22.

5. Referring to the illustration on page 108, arrange the squares around the quilt. Join the squares to make the outer border strips, placing a 2" x 2½" rectangle in the center of each top and bottom strip and a 1" x 2½" rectangle in the center of each side strip.

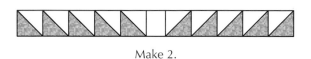

Make 2.

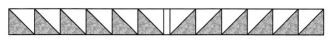

Make 2.

6. Sew the side outer border strips to the quilt top, then add the top and bottom border strips.

QUILT FINISHING

1. Layer the quilt top with batting and backing; baste.
2. Quilt by machine or by hand.
3. From the dark blue print, cut 4 strips, each 2½" wide. Press strips in half lengthwise; bind the quilt.

DESIGNING QUILTS WITH ANIMAL BLOCKS

I hope you will use these blocks in your own way, in your own quilts. Following are some thoughts you may find useful as you design original quilts.

Using Single Blocks

The quickest and easiest way to make a quilt is to add strips or borders to a single block. There are many ways of doing this:

- Add border strips cut from the background fabric, as in Robyn Oats's Elephant quilt on page 42. Bind the edges with a contrasting color or value.
- Add borders with straight-cut corners, as in the Donkey quilt on page 21, or with mitered corners, as in the Camel quilt on page 43.
- Include a narrow inner border, as in the Toucan quilt on page 23.
- Add some corner squares, as in the Koala quilt on page 25.
- Add simple pieced borders, as in the Scotty Dog quilt on page 35 and the Parrot quilt on page 36.
- Use theme fabric to turn the block into a picture, as in the Owl quilt on page 18.
- Add border strips in a log-cabin fashion, as in the Loon quilt on page 28.

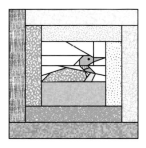

- Make crazy-pieced borders, as in the Rabbit quilt on page 20.

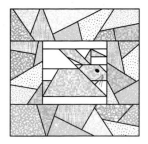

- Set the block on point, as in the Blue Jay quilt on page 31. The on-point set is easy to make. First, make four quarter-square triangles from background fabric by cutting a square the same size as the animal block (finished size) plus 1¼". Cut this square *twice* on the diagonal, then sew the triangles around the block. Second, make four half-square triangles from border fabric by cutting two squares the same size as the animal block (finished size) plus ⅞". Cut these squares *once* on the diagonal, then sew the triangles around the block. In both cases, determine the size to cut the squares (from which to cut triangles) from the finished size of the block.

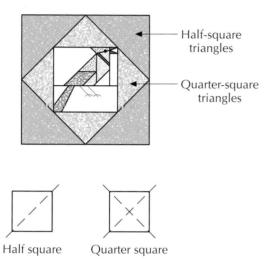

Half-square triangles

Quarter-square triangles

Half square   Quarter square

Using Repetition

Pattern is created through repetition, an important tool in quilt design. Repeating and reversing (making a mirror image) of the block creates interest, as in Miaow Cats on page 19 and the Penguin quilt on page 40. Another creative idea is to change the scale of the block using a photocopier. For an example, see Penguin Beach on page 41.

Combining Blocks with Other Patchwork

A great way to make quilts is to combine animal blocks with other patchwork.
- Use the animal block as part of a traditional pieced block, such as placing the Buffalo in the center of a Navajo block (page 29).
- Combine an animal or multiple animal block(s) with traditional blocks, as in the Hummingbird quilt on page 33 and the Dolphin quilt on page 30. *Note:* To be successful, the animal block and the traditional blocks have to be compatible in size and design.
- Use an animal block with another theme block, as in the Bear in the Woods quilt on page 45. (The bear is combined with a pieced tree.) The Black Bear block was extended with background fabric to make it the same size as the tree blocks.
- Use traditional patchwork blocks as alternate blocks, as in the North American Animals quilt on page 46.

Combining Different Animal Blocks

Combining different animal blocks in one quilt creates some special problems because the animals are usually different sizes in real life, but in the blocks they are all 4". (If you put the animals into what the viewer reads as the same space, they could look odd—a bear and a Canada goose the same size?) To keep the animals from looking odd, give each its own space:
- Surround each animal with one or more borders, as in the Farm quilt on page 44.
- Separate the animals with sashing strips, as in the Australian Animals quilt on page 47.
- Use alternate blocks to create space around each animal block, as in the North American Animals quilt on page 46.

METRIC CONVERSION

- The animal blocks are all 4" square, or slightly more than 10cm. Rather than converting the blocks, use them as is, then trim to 10cm plus seam allowances. For metric sewing, seam allowances should be 0.75cm (7.5mm).
- To rotary-cut squares, rectangles, and strips that include 0.75cm seam allowances, add 1.5cm to the finished measurements.

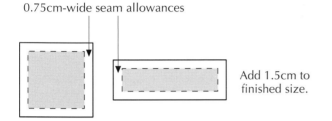

0.75cm-wide seam allowances

Add 1.5cm to finished size.

- To rotary cut half-square triangles that include 0.75cm scam allowanccs, cut a squarc that is 2.5cm larger than the short sides of the finished triangle. Cut the square once diagonally to yield 2 triangles.

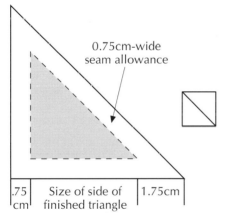

0.75cm-wide seam allowance

.75 cm | Size of side of finished triangle | 1.75cm

= size of side of finished triangle plus 2.5cm

- To rotary cut quarter-square triangles that include 0.75cm seam allowances, cut a square that is 3.5cm larger than the long side of the finished triangle. Cut the square twice diagonally to yield 4 triangles.

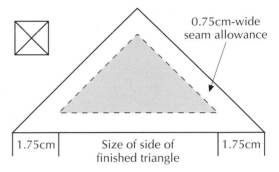

0.75cm-wide seam allowance

1.75cm | Size of side of finished triangle | 1.75cm

= size of side of finished triangle plus 3.5cm

TABLE OF USEFUL METRIC EQUIVALENTS FOR PATCHWORK

NOTE: This table does not give exact equivalents; the numbers have been rounded up or down to the nearest useful metric equivalent. When two metric measurements are given, choose the most convenient size.

¼"	=	0.75cm (7.5mm)
½"	=	1cm
	or	1.5cm *when you are adding two 0.75cm seam allowances*
¾"	–	2cm
1"	=	2.5cm
1¼"	=	3cm
1½"	=	4cm
2"	=	5cm
2½"	=	6cm
3"	=	8cm
4"	=	10cm
5"	=	12cm
6"	=	15cm or 16cm
9" (¼ yd.)	=	24cm
12"	=	30cm or 32cm
18" (½ yd.)	=	48cm
36" (1 yd.)	=	90cm
40"	=	100cm (1m)

MEET THE AUTHOR

Margaret Rolfe, an Australian quiltmaker, has had a lifelong interest in patchwork and quilting. She was inspired to make quilting her own craft after living in the United States for several months in 1975. At that time, the American Bicentennial was approaching, and quilting was about to be discovered by American women as an exciting craft with a rich past and a great creative future. After returning to Australia, Margaret combined the knowledge she had gleaned in the United States with a lot of learning by trial and error and began to make her own quilts.

During the 1980s, Margaret started to create original quilt designs. Her first were quilts of Australian wild flowers and wildlife. She found pieced blocks most intriguing, and her experimentation led to her unique approach to patchwork design and sewing.

Margaret's designs have been published in a series of books, including *Australian Patchwork Designs, Quilt a Koala,* and *Patchwork Quilts to Make for Children.* Her interest in history is reflected in her book *Patchwork Quilts in Australia.*

Go Wild with Quilts, her first book of pieced patterns for North American wildlife, was a result of Margaret's five-year stay in Canada in the late 1960s, as well as many trips to the United States and Canada since then. The success of this book and Margaret's continuing creation of new animal and bird designs led to *Go Wild with Quilts—Again!*

In this book, *A Quilter's Ark*, Margaret has adapted many of her animal and bird designs into small blocks made with quick and easy foundation-piecing techniques.

Margaret's quilting career is enthusiastically supported by her scientist husband, Barry, and her three grown-up children, Bernard, Phil, and Melinda.